CRABBIT OLD BUGGERS

An A-Z of Unreasonableness, Stubbornness and the Determination Never to be Impressed by Anything

JOHN K V EUNSON

BLACK & WHITE PUBLISHING

First published 2006
by Black & White Publishing Ltd
99 Giles Street, Edinburgh EH6 6BZ

ISBN 10:   1 84502 108 8
ISBN 13: 978 1 84502 108 5

British Library Cataloguing in Publication Data:
A catalogue record for this book is available
from the British Library.

Printed and bound by Nørhaven Paperback A/S

CONTENTS

DEDICATION

This book is dedicated to COBs, to everyone with COB tendencies, especially family, friends and Margaret McShane's lovely daughter, and to those who have to live and work with them.

INTRODUCTION

Never mind your grumpy old men and your grumpy old women and the TV shows with forty-something millionaire celebrities wittering on about how good life used to be in the good old days. A far more interesting section of society are your Crabbit Old Buggers.

Crabbit Old Buggers, or COBs for short, are not defined by gender, nationality or creed. In fact Crabbit Old Buggers are not defined by age, as for every jolly pensioner there is an exceptionally grim teenager. Although it must be said that, as with a good corked wine, maturity and life experience allows our COBs to achieve even greater levels of crabbitness.

Crabbit Old Buggers are dour, intolerant, stubborn and unreasonable. To be a Crabbit Old Bugger is a state of mind, a way of living, a reason to exist that transcends all and an overriding determination never to be impressed by anything or anyone. For COBs, the future is not bright, but just something that has to be endured. And endure it they will, and my God will they make sure that the rest of us know all about it.

Crabbit Old Buggers, the book, is an A-Z of the subjects that most exercise our COBs and looks at what makes us crabbit, how crabbit we can get about different issues in our lives and why sometimes, just sometimes, a little bit of COB in all of us is no bad thing.

TEN COB COMMANDMENTS
The essential guidelines of Cobbery

1) Thou shalt never willingly be told what to do.
2) Thou shalt not approve of any modern art or of installations involving cows.
3) Thou shalt not say bad things about Michael Palin.
4) Remember the Sabbath Day and make sure you get your free DVD with your Sunday paper.
5) Honour thy father and thy mother, but no more than absolutely necessary.
6) Thou shalt not wear shorts in public.
7) Thou shalt not flirt with anybody – including your partner.
8) Thou shalt never lend anything just in case you do not get it back.
9) Thou shalt not bear false witness against thy neighbour, but if you catch them using an illegal hosepipe they will face your wrath.
10) Thou shalt not covet thy neighbour, thy neighbour's wife, thy neighbours ass or thy neighbours wife's ass – but to be honest those jeans do not really do her any favours.

A COB CALENDAR

The essential elements of each long year

JANUARY – Another bloody year. A time of freezing temperatures, freezing pipes and no daylight for days on end.

FEBRUARY – More rain, more snow, more biting winds and more Christmas bills to be paid. The only consolation about February is that there are only 28 days.

MARCH – Still wet, still windy, still cold. To all intents and purposes still winter. Ever more virulent viruses and flus sweep the nation coinciding remarkably with a fifth of the nation deciding it is time to take a week off. Three swans die of food poisoning and the nation grinds to a halt.

APRIL – On the one hand, spring flowers and lambs with gambolling habits. On the other, the acute anticlimax that is the low chocolate to packaging ratio of Easter eggs. Not forgetting the now insistent call for long-promised home improvements/decorating/upgrading/renovations to be backed up by more than buying a couple of paint tester pots from B&Q.

MAY – Almost tolerable as months go if it was not for the ridiculous amount of bank holidays and the weekend transport and IKEA hell that ensues, coupled with the annual disappointment of yet another mediocre football season where talent and skill come a distant second to how many billions one spends.

JUNE – Is that really half the year gone? How depressing.

JULY – Now uncomfortably hot and muggy as drought and global warming kick in. Swarms of bored kids on their summer holidays, wasps and midges ravage the nation. Nothing on TV except six foot ten East European tennis players of both sexes grunting.

AUGUST – That will be the end of the summer then. Shops full of tourists queuing for stamps and the roads clogged with mile-long tailbacks behind three clapped-out caravans from Wales.

SEPTEMBER – Time for the fortnightly annual

holiday and the joys of airport delays, heatstroke and herds of sunburnt Brits displaying their tattoos and deep-fried stomachs.

OCTOBER – Temperature drops ten degrees. Walking made difficult by force ten gales. Trains stop running because of leaves on track. Christmas products on sale in shops for months now. The sheer pleasure of Halloween where gangs of children roam around demanding money with menaces and everybody else thinks dressing up as a psychotic chainsaw serial murderer is incredibly amusing.

NOVEMBER – Dark. Wet. Windy. Little in the way of redeeming features other than a good bowl of soup.

DECEMBER – One long, expensive build-up to having to eat brussels sprouts again. Numerous drunken works nights out to avoid at all costs. Finding yourself for no apparent reason eating huge amounts of what used to be called tangerines.

THE A-Z OF COBs

A

A 4x4

Hummers, Jeep Grand Cherokees, Land Rover Discoveries – sports utility vehicles in other words. Perfectly acceptable if you are bringing sustenance to starving Cheviots in the Highlands or chasing kangaroos and cane toads in the Australian Outback, but as an environmentally unsound, fuel inefficient vehicle to take young Marcus and Ophelia to nursery before popping into town for a skinny latte and organic houmous shopping, they are quite ridiculous – especially when driven by women so small that they need a leg-up to get in the driver's seat.

ACCIDENTS

Statistically most accidents happen in the house in the North East of England, take place on a Sunday and happen to 27-year-olds. COBs avoid such accidents by keeping clear of young people, taking the dog for long walks at the weekends and steering clear of Newcastle as much as possible.

AGRICULTURE

Farming is an occupation long associated with COBs. Working outdoors in all seasons and weather for hours on end with only Bobby the faithful Border Collie for company has never produced the most garrulous and avuncular of men and women. Furthermore poor seasons, poor sales, low profits and no holidays make farming an industry that as many people escape from as want to join. When you add, in the last decade, the effects of BSE, foot and mouth disease, avian flu and being regularly screwed by our friendly supermarket chains, it is not surprising that only hardcore COBs are left to grumble about the price of wool.

AIR TRAVEL

As most of us travel the globe in search of new countries, new lands, new cultures and experiences – before they all disappear because more of us are travelling the globe looking for them – it is important to mention the joys of air travel.

Never mind the delays, the waiting around, the lack of leg-room, the annoying brats kicking the back of your seat, the likelihood of it being another bloody Ben Stiller film that they show and the never-explained question of what is the point of the brace position.

No, what COBs cannot abide is the sheer stupidity of people queuing to board when they have allocated seats, the rush to get out of your seats before the plane has even come to a halt as if that is ever going to get you out of the airport any quicker, the no smoking light being switched off as if there is ever going to be a chance of being able to light up in the first place and why oh why oh why if drunken, abusive passengers are such a danger to air travel do airlines insist on filling people with booze for hours on end as soon as they sit down.

AMERICA

Long before George W. Bush, COBs have had a historical antipathy to the USA – at least since they rode to the rescue in the Second World War to save us all and take over the world with their chewing gum, fizzy drink, appalling spelling and even more appalling golfwear.

So for all of the Marshall Plan that economically

reconstructed Europe, the classic movies, the great music, *Cheers*, *Friends* and *The Simpsons*, as far as COBs are concerned America is still the brash, insular, arrogant, neurotic nation they have always been, who will one day probably blow us all up without meaning to. Not that COBS have any truck with the whole American-Evil-Empire, Fidel-Castro-is-a-saint, let's-all-drink-rum-and-salsa theory of world politics. As far as they are concerned Americans are not bad but just have serious size issues.

ART

COBs have strong opinions on art. They have nothing against art galleries but never think of visiting one. COBs also have nothing against people spending their spare time painting landscapes, portraits, boats and, if they must, bowls of fruit but would be unlikely to pay money to buy one.

The ultimate cruelty to inflict on a COB would be to make them spend days on end in a modern art gallery, enjoying the merits and aesthetics of huge canvasses with a big stripe of blue across it, half a dozen tyres strewn across a floor, a video of a light being switched on and off again and some installation of metal, papier mache and baked beans representing the sanctity of womanhood.

As far as COBs are concerned, they know they are deliberately being wound up with all of this modern art nonsense, but still cannot stop themselves from using the phrase: 'a three-year-old could do that'.

ASTROLOGY

Any person who allows Russell Grant and Mystic Meg to effect their lives in any way whatsoever deserves everything they get as far as COBs are concerned.

An alternative view of the zodiac

AQUARIUS
Water carrier. Useful person in a drought.

ARIES
Ram. Curly-haired – tends to sleep around once a year.

CANCER
Crab. Likes going to the beach.

CAPRICORN
Goat. Only seen these days in Mediterranean art-house films.

LEO
Lion. Likes steak, preferably rare.

LIBRA. Scales. Found in bathrooms. Deemed
untrustworthy by many.

PISCES
Fish. A lot less of them than there used to be.
Goes best with peas.

SAGITTARIUS
Archer. Not to be trusted.

SCORPIO
Scorpion. Prone to wind (of change that is).

TAURUS
Bull. Faster than you think. Not to be provoked.

VIRGO
Virgin. Dependable sacrificial victim in satanic
ritual. Like fish, less of them about.

GEMINI
Twins. Eurovision Song Contest – nul points.

In other words – all complete and utter tosh

B

BABIES

COBs do not tend to bond especially well with babies. When confronted with young Chardonnay or Pablo, Merlin or Nebuchadnezzar and their delighted parents, COBs immediate instinct is to get as far away as possible. And to the unlikely question of do you want to hold the baby, the COB's answer is always, why?

BANKS

COBs hate modern banks. Not enough tellers, dreadful furniture, their obsession with sitting down when all you want to do is be out of there in two minutes and, as for dress-down Friday – do you really trust these people to take care of your money?

And that's if you still have a bank to go to, as one by one they are all turned into huge megapubs with two-for-one Bacardi breezers deals and populated with groups of young men wearing identical Top Shop shirts. So you end up on the phone, pressing an endless series of buttons which much like the TV series *Lost* promise much but never actually achieve the ultimate goal – which is either getting off the island or actually speaking to a real human being in the same time zone as yourself.

And as for cashline machines, is there anything more infuriating than, after searching for ages for a machine that works, having it then inform you there will be a £1.50 charge. No wonder so many get broken.

BARBECUES

COBs are highly suspicious of barbecues as they view their announcement as a precursor to an afternoon of guaranteed rain.

Also, fundamentally, what is the point of barbecues? Once you have stuffed yourself with two burgers, politely commented on how nice the potato salad is and witnessed the excitement of grown men watching sausages cook slowly for an hour – what exactly are you supposed to do?

TONY BLAIR

Much like with that other fading British icon of the last decade, David Beckham, COBs were never convinced about Tony Blair in the first place. Shiny, earnest sincerity and never-ending grinning were never qualities that were likely to win them over. And to be honest, Labour would have won the 1997 election anyway if John Smith had lived or Gordon Brown had been leader – anything to end 18 years of Tory rule and the charismatic premiership of John Major. So, unlike all the other poor suckers who voted for New Labour in 1997, at least COBs cannot claim to be disillusioned, as they expected the worst all along.

The consolation of course is that, like Thatcher and Major, one day sometime soon, Tony will no longer be Prime Minister and he and Cherie can head into the sunset, perpetually travelling the world playing tennis with Silvio Berlusconi and making millions on the lecture circuit. However, a word of warning. Please remember that, after a decade of Tony and everything he has done and said, just because he now says he will definitely stand down before the next election does not actually mean that he is going to do it.

BLIND DATES

Even worse than the prospect of a COB being made to go on a date, is a COB being made to go on a blind date. Unless the blind date in question turns out to be either Penelope Cruz, Nigella Lawson, Clive Owen or Denise Van Outen, then your COB is going to look disappointed no matter how attractive or pleasant the person may be.

This is why dating agencies and the internet are so helpful in avoiding such situations, for, give or take a decade or two, when meeting for the first time both parties have a vague idea about what to expect.

In particular COBs are suspicious of possible dates who on their resumé claim to have a Good Sense Of Humour, as in reality this usually means somebody who drinks too much, talks incessantly and laughs at their own jokes. Even worse are dates who claim to be warm and cuddly and possessing a GSOH, as they will drink too much, talk incessantly, laugh at their own jokes and be likely not to have seen their feet for several years when standing up.

The desire for quieter types partly explains the popularity of Eastern Europeans and Asians as possible partners, as having little English is seen by COBs as being a distinct advantage.

BOOTS

On the rare occasions when they give it any thought, COBs are somewhat baffled by what young people wear today. That teenage Goths (bless them) are still the height of counter-culture thirty years after Siouxsie Sioux is strangely reassuring. The wearing of Ramones T-shirts by people who have never heard 'Blitzkrieg Bop' on the other hand is just plain wrong. COBs are all in favour of the fashion for giant belts, not because they like them especially, but because anything that covers up excessive midriffs is to be welcomed.

Most inexplicable, however, is the rise of Ugg and their furry-booted ilk. Looking ludicrous enough at the best of times, the equivalent of wearing comedy slippers outdoors, wet weather makes them truly ridiculous as you end up wearing bedraggled poodles on your feet.

BOSSES

There are pros and cons of having a COB as a boss. On the downside you should never expect any praise for your work and the chances of raises, bonuses and lavish Christmas night-outs are somewhat limited. However, being positive, with a COB as a boss you always know where you stand, expectations never change and such phrases as team-building, motivation, career development and strategic planning are thankfully never mentioned.

BOXING

COBs are quite fond of the noble sport of men inflicting severe physical injury on the heads of their opponents with all proceeds going to the brave promoters who fix the events in the first place.

Having said that, COBs have not actually watched a fight since Frank Bruno lost on points to a Land of Leather sofa and think Joe Calzaghe was the guy who got to number one with 'Shaddap You Face'.

COBs think women boxing is intrinsically wrong and it makes them quite squeamish. Curiously, on the other hand, women wrestling is seen as surprisingly enjoyable.

BOY & GIRL BANDS

Now you used to know where you were with boy and girl bands:

The Monkees – Peter, Davy, Mickey and the one with the hat.

The Bay City Rollers – Les, Woody, Eric and the other two.

Take That – Robbie, Gary, Mark, Orange and the one that nobody remembers.

And *The Spice Girls* – Posh, Baby, Sporty, genuinely Scary and downright bonkers.

But nowadays? Can anyone tell Boyzone and Westlife apart? More importantly, can anyone remember a single one of their songs? Was there anybody else in Atomic Kitten other than Kerry Katona's breasts? Who were Five and Blue again?

And as for Girls Aloud, why have they not split up yet? Why are there so many of them? And what is the attraction of going out with multi-millionaire footballers anyway? On the positive side, however, wasn't it nice that they asked their freckly pal to join the group?

C

THE CABINET

Is there anything more disheartening than discovering at the beginning of *Question Time* that one of the panellists is Patricia Hewitt? Can anyone talk more slowly and in a more consistently patronising manner? Close runners-up in the worst member of the Cabinet competition are the scary cyborgs Ruth Kelly and Hazel Blears, the Stewart-Granger-swallows-a-wasp impersonator that is Peter Hain, the cold-blooded assassin's eyes of Dr John Reid and the irrepressibly earnest eternal teenager Douglas Alexander. No wonder David Dimbleby gets irritable some weeks.

CALL CENTRES

A dislike of cold calling is certainly not the preserve of COBs, but COBs get especially irritated by the sheer illogicality of it. Why would somebody want to buy their gas from an electricity company or electricity from a gas company? Why would you want to join a phone company that calls you on a dreadful line and has a five second delay before somebody speaks to you? Why if you are interested in travelling abroad would you agree to go to the outskirts of Stirling to pick up your free prize – don't they have post there? Why is there always a kitchen promotion in your area – how can one street be that lucky?

And why oh why are there only ever two questions that they want to ask? How uninquisitive can these people be?

CARTOONS

COBs can get surprisingly worked up by cartoons. They have never found Mickey Mouse, Pluto or the Road Runner going Beep Bloody Beep funny in the slightest and are happy to tell you about this at length. Furthermore, the mere mention of the *All New Tom and Jerry* and *All New Pink Panther Show* can still make them apoplectic with rage. And that is before we even mention the Patrick Kielty of cartoon characters, Scrappy Doo, the psychological trauma of whose appearance decades ago is still something that COBs cannot bring themselves to talk about.

CELEBRITIES

It is difficult to conclude which celebrity COBs most dislike. George Galloway MP is an obvious candidate, but is too unsubtle a provocateur to be taken seriously and if anything it is the thousands of people who keep re-electing him that one wonders about. Noel Edmonds is too desperate to be liked. Jonny Vaughan and Chris Evans kept making TV programmes so dreadful that you never see them anymore. Gordon Ramsay shows promise as his innate lack of humour becomes more and more apparent and Nikki Campbell has an ego so huge and a manner so patronising that you are never quite sure if the shows he presents are serious or a post-ironic spoof.

However, when all is said and done, there is one celebrity who consistently, over two decades, has got more COBs' backs up than anyone else, with a persona so hectoring, so condescending, so lacking in human warmth and so downright unfunny that despite being a comedian, a writer, a novelist, a lyricist, a presenter, a friend of royalty and of Andrew Lloyd Webber – the award to the celebrity COBs simply cannot abide goes unanimously to Sir Ben Elton OBE.

CELEBRITY CHEFS

Nothing wrong with Delia – boiler of eggs and Norwich City cheerleader. But is there really any need for Ainsley Harriot (the Kriss Akabussi of cookery), Gary Rhodes with his twenty-years-too-late haircut and Anthony Worrall Thompson (Hobbit extra from Lord Of the Rings)?

Not that COBs would ever watch a cookery programme on TV. They either know it all already or the kitchen is alien land where the fridge lives.

CHARITY

COBs are all for charity. They will spend large portions of their day frequenting the ever expanding charity shop market – which, along with Greggs, will soon be all that is left of retail in the high streets of Britain's market towns.

What COBs cannot be doing with as far as charity is concerned is events such as Children In Need and Comic Relief. It is one thing to be subjected to emotional blackmail with the subtlety of a red-nosed sledgehammer, but quite another to have sit through hours of BBC newsreaders singing karaoke and the cast of *Casualty* performing Wagner's Ring Cycle.

At least with the telethons you know what they

are and are given plenty of warning to make alternative plans for the evening, but with Live 8 and Bob Geldof demanding we give him our fooking awareness and in the meantime here's Sting – what was that all about exactly?

CHEESE

COBs like cheese. Jarlsberg, Edam, Brie, Wensleydale, Cheddar etc, as long as its not one of those whiffy runny blues. In fact COBs, despite themselves, are suckers for a good cheeseboard and will rarely if ever say that they are beyond cheese – or any of the rest of Destiny's Child for that matter.

CHINESE FOOD

As far as COBs are concerned Chinese food is much like a TV Christmas special, a new James Bond movie and ten-pin bowling – never as good as you think it is going to be.

CHRISTMAS

The turkey, the sprouts, the family, the giving, the receiving, the wilting tree, the hyperactive children, the inexplicable consumption of mulled wine, the sheer horror of mistletoe and the consistent disappointment of seasonal TV specials – nothing is more underwhelming than the celebration of the birth of our Lord. To make matters worse for COBs they can always predict what their presents are going to be each year – socks, the *Oor Wullie* or *The Broons* annual and a selection box of dates and selected dried fruit.

As far as COBs are concerned, Christmas Day would be the most turgid, depressing day of the year if it was not for the sheer misery of New Year's Eve six days later.

CINEMA

COBs hate going to the cinema. You have the expensive, excessive, unhealthy snacks that make you ill. You have the hours and hours of adverts trying to persuade you that Southern Comfort is not actually the most god-awful drink imaginable. And, when the film finally starts if it is not ear-splittingly loud then you have the noise of people eating, slurping, chatting, turning up late, going to the toilet halfway through and keeping their bloody phone switched on.

More than all that, it is the sitting next to complete strangers that COBs cannot abide. They are also not that fond of people sitting behind them staring at their hairline. There are therefore only two possible seats left in the entire cinema for a COB to feel comfortable in, extreme back left and extreme back right – and the view from both is terrible.

CITY BREAKS

City-breaks have become an increasingly popular way for COBs to travel on holiday. They can visit the Gaudi architecture of Barcelona, the Charles Bridge of Prague, the canals of Amsterdam and the numerous sights and antiquities of the Eternal City of Rome, all without spending a fortune or taking more than a couple of days off work.

The shortness of such holidays also means that time for shopping is mercifully curtailed and you don't need to pack more than 3 pairs of pants.

COLD WAR

Despite the occasional pleasure of a pint of Staropramen, COBs of both a left- and right-leaning persuasion miss the Cold War. They were happy days when you knew where you were, knew who the enemy was and had plenty of fine John Le Carré spy thrillers to enjoy. All you had to worry about was the

East Germans always winning the athletics and imminent nuclear apocalypse.

COLLECTABLES

COBs like collecting. From football stickers and toy pigs to Toby jugs and the complete works of Leonard Cohen, COBs are prone to their little obsessions that can last decades and take up a third of the house.

That is why COBs are so grateful for eBay and the internet, for liberating them from the hours and hours of trawling through hundreds and hundreds of hatchbacks at car boot sales in the vain hope of finding the famous 1973 *Blue Peter Annual* with Lesley Judd wearing hot pants on the cover.

THE COMMONWEALTH

Probably the strangest international organisation in the world where membership appears to depend on celebrating the fact that at one stage you were invaded, conquered, economically exploited or had native populations massacred. Stranger still is the recent addition to the Commonwealth of countries such as Cameroon and Mozambique who were never ever ruled by the British, but are hopeful that

Margaret Beckett will invade sometime soon.

COBs are quite supportive of the Commonwealth. Many of them have relatives who settled in Australia, New Zealand and Canada and it is reassuring to know that they are so many thousands of miles away and will only visit every ten years or so. Furthermore, the Commonwealth Games every four years must be reassuring for the Isle Of Man as a way to remind people that they still exist.

COMEDIANS

Despite everything, COBs do profess to having a sense of humour. Under thorough investigation, however, this love of comedy appears to go no further than the 1970s and the work of Morecambe and Wise, The Two Ronnies and Dave Allen. Or, to be accurate, the half a dozen clips (fork handles, Andre Previn, etc) that get constantly repeated on compilation TV shows annoyingly presented by Jimmy Carr. COBs also used to like Billy Connolly before he turned into the tiresome millionaire COB that we know today.

COBs have certainly chortled or chuckled at the television since 1979, but sadly they cannot remember when.

COMPUTERS

You tend not to find COBs in IT departments. Not only are they unlikely to wear comedy T-shirts and may perhaps be lacking in the people skills to help distraught and traumatised colleagues when the e-mail is down for five minutes or their laptops can't download the new Zutons album, but, more importantly, the temptation for COBs to physically dismantle all computers component by component, accompanied by industrial strength language, when switching on and off doesn't work would just be too strong.

COMPUTER GAMES

COBs total knowledge of computer games is that there was a beeping tennis game around 1978.

CONSERVATIVES

COBs have always instinctively disliked the Tories for their smug golf club, G&T, money-grabbing snobbery. Nothing used to reinforce this view more than if you saw two or more Young Conservatives in the same room. This has made the electoral collapse of the Tories in the last 10 years difficult for COBs, as it was always good to know your enemy. Under William Hague and Ian Duncan Smith they became so inconsequential that you almost felt sorry for them.

But lo, salvation is upon us. New Tories have risen again and for all David Cameron's love of Morrissey and bicycling green-tinged rebranding – class war, political hatred, economic collapse and a divided nation will soon be upon us. Hoorah.

CREDIT CARDS

COBs are not the greatest users of credit cards. While they have their uses, they prefer to use real money wherever possible. You know where you are with cash and COBs cannot comprehend people who have dozens of different debit cards in their wallet. How do they keep track of everything? How do they remember all those different pin numbers? And can you really use your library card in Safeways?

CRICKET

The lovely and noble spot of cricket has a high percentage of COB followers. They are attracted by the tradition, the history, the cakes, the sweet sound of willow on leather on a summers afternoon in between the hours and hours of no play due to rain and bad light. They like the fact that matches can last five days, seven hours a day and you still don't have a winner. And that it still matters that in 1948 Sir Don Bradman ended up four runs short of having a test average of 100.

Cricket COBs are not fans, however, of one day cricket or the office quickie that is 20-20 cricket. These games are nowhere near long enough, far too many runs are scored, pyjamas should never be worn outdoors and you would never catch Geoffrey Boycott hitting a good length ball out of the ground for six.

CRIME

As far as COBs are concerned all crime in the UK is perpetrated by younger members of society wearing hooded tops. Which also includes wearers of baseball caps, improbably white trainers and generally greasy hair.

The ideal solution to deal with hoodies as far as COBs are concerned would be specially-built young persons' shopping centres where youths can slouch, swagger, shout unintelligible abuse and happyslap each other to their hearts' content, leaving the rest of us in peace.

CRUISES

If COBs are forced to go on holiday for a period longer than a city break, then cruises are becoming an increasingly popular option. On the plus side, you have all your food and drink prepared for you, you can sit in the sun all day and you can have daily excursions to the most beautiful locations in the Mediterranean and the Caribbean. On the negative side however, there is no escape from either the boat or the people on the boat, there is compulsory cabaret every night and the average age of holidaymaker on board is so high there is always the concern that if you died while at sea would anybody actually notice?

CYCLING

Cycling is a noble, practical and environmentally sound pastime that even David Cameron and Boris Johnson cannot make unfashionable. However, it is not New Labour Tories, nor cyclists sneaking through traffic and jumping lights, nor even those ridiculous cycling helmets that annoy the COBs most about cyclists, but those unfeasibly tight and shockingly vivid cycling shorts which, when stretched across inappropriate physiques, can be disturbing in the extreme.

D

DANCING

'I Bet You Look Good On the Dancefloor' by the Arctic Monkeys is not a tune that you will see many COBs getting on down to. Furthermore 'I Bet You Look Good On The Dancefloor' is not a statement that can ever be said about COBs, as frankly they cannot dance.

An early indication of crabbitness can be identified in teenage years by an inability to move either hips or shoulders no matter what popular beat combo are playing. From Blondie to the Stones, the Pogues to the Prodigy, Donna Summer to the Buena Vista Social Club – you will witness the same rigid side to side shuffle with hands clenched below the chest at all times and intense concentration at avoiding all possible eye contact. The ultimate nightmare scenario is of course being dragged up to a song you hate, the girl wanders off and you end up in the hell of all hells where your nearest dancers are all men and they are playing the twelve inch dance mix.

As the years go by and the music gets louder,

dancing is abandoned altogether with numerous excuses proffered when asked to dance ranging from a bad back, wrong type of shoes or the more common feigning deafness and ignoring the request altogether.

There is, of course, one exception to the no dancing rule which you will unfortunately witness at all weddings when the worst dancers in the world inexplicably feel obliged to get up for Shania Twain and carnage ensues.

DATING

If COBs found themselves reluctantly in the position of dating, then the question is not how many dates it takes before you are likely to get some action, but how many dates it is going to take before stopping having to pay for everything.

DEPRESSION

COBs don't have time for depression, they are too busy concentrating on being bitter and twisted to have time to start feeling sorry for themselves.

DOGS

Nothing wrong with proper dogs. Intelligent, bonnie working dogs such as Labradors or collies or big stupid slobbery dogs such as retrievers, hounds and spaniels. But as for those yappy toy dogs and terriers being carried around by women of a certain age with matching ribbons in their hair, they should either be squashed, have their larynx removed or both. And as for Labradoodles and their designer mutant ilk – where is it going to end? A shih-tzu crossed with a boxer to give you an Audley Harrison or a cocker crossed with a mastiff to give you a dog in constant heat?

DRIVING

COBs are, as a rule, very good drivers. The main supporters for this statement are of course COBs themselves, but there is some justification behind this claim. Firstly, COBs tend to like driving. It can be a safe haven away from the hells of home, work, family and general mankind. The open road, the comfortable leather, the powerful engine responding to your every whim, Radio 2 or Talk Radio tuned in to exactly the right volume – our COBs could nearly be called happy.

The problem is everybody else on the road. The boy racers, the Sunday pensioners, the 4x4 road hogs, the sports car flash gits, the buses, the taxis, the delivery vans, the caravans, the cyclists, drivers that don't indicate, drivers that pull out without looking, drivers that jump lights, drivers that sit at lights whilst checking their makeup, drivers that go too fast, drivers that go too slow, drivers that overtake blind, drivers that don't let you out and drivers who require a space the size of North Wales to be able to park properly.

With so many of the motoring population dismissed as being simply not competent enough to be on the road, every journey is a possible minefield with pitfalls and ineptitude at every corner. It is therefore no wonder that COBs are good drivers, as they have to concentrate like hawks to avoid all this potential mayhem. As the old saying goes, just because you are paranoid does not mean that somebody is not trying to drive you off the road.

When all is said and done, however, it is definitely better that COBs stay on the road. No matter how crabbit they get when driving, it is as nothing to the sheer misery of a COB on public transport or, even worse, being driven by somebody else.

DRUGS

COBs are not your typical illicit drug-takers – the illegality and the loss of self-control are not for them. Furthermore, COBs can often be heard vehemently condemning the evils of drugs, people who take drugs, and the people who make money out of drugs, as they drink their pint, sip their nip and puff away on their Benson & Hedges.

E

EATING OUT

When taking a COB out for dinner the first thing to remind them is that going out for a Chinese, Thai, Vietnamese or Japanese is not to be referred to as having a 'Chinky' and that cat is unlikely to be on the menu.

Other points to remember when taking a COB out are that ambience and atmosphere will be less important than the time taken to get your food. That they will be suspicious of all sauce that is not brown or tartar. That they will only tip if service of a mythical level of perfection is provided. And in these days of cosmopolitan, international, innovative, quality cuisine, the only starters they will ever consider ordering are the prawn cocktail or the soup.

Finally, if you take a COB out for dinner, don't expect either a raucous evening or even a dessert, as they will want to be home by 9.30 at the latest.

EDINBURGH

The capital of Scotland is famous for many things. Its historic castle and palace, the Georgian grandeur of the New Town, the international arts festival, the famous writers who have lived there from Robert Louis Stevenson and Arthur Conan Doyle to Irvine Welsh and J.K. Rowling, for being the Athens of the North or the Reykjavik of the South.

Edinburgh is also known as being a bastion of reserve, tradition, commerce and the Establishment, where you will always have had you tea and, in the days when we had a mining industry, sex was what the coal came in.

Not surprisingly Edinburgh is full of COBs.

THE ELDERLY

No matter how old your COBs might be – they never classify themselves as elderly. That twilight zone of personal care, residential housing, meals on wheels and old folks' homes is a world that, as with modern pop and computer games, should be ignored as much as possible. And as for the saying 'one foot in the grave', well that has got nothing to do with age, as COBs will always point out that death is but a runaway bus or fishbone away.

ELECTIONS

There are some COBs who justify not voting by the often-repeated philosophy that politicians are all the same and voting only encourages them. On the whole, however, COBs believe in the democratic process and come rain or shine will use their franchise at general, local and European elections, as well as Sports Personality of the Year. In fact the more local the elections the better as there is always some diddy councillor to vote out, some other candidate to have a feud with and numerous opportunities to personally raise the question of dog shite and paper recycling bins. Not that COBs would ever actually stand as candidates (no matter how tempting that might seem) as that would mean talking to people and smiling on a regular basis.

ELEPHANTS

It was the veteran Chinese Foreign Minister Chou En Lai who was asked in 1972 what he thought had been the influence on the world of the 1789 French Revolution and said that it was far too early to say.

Now if ever there was a group of serious COBs, then we are talking about octogenerian Chinese Communist leaders, but the basic principle still applies that it takes a COB to bemoan the fall of the Ottoman Empire, to care if the ball crossed the line in 1966, to remember when Cliff Richard used to have sex, to blame Margaret Thatcher for stopping free milk to school children and to just about recall when New Labour were not new and actually were vaguely Labour.

It is always said that it is good to forgive and forget – COBs do neither.

THE EUROPEAN UNION

The European Union (or, as older COBs insist on calling it, the Common Market) has never been one of the COBs' favourite organisations.

Not that they have anything against peace in Europe, European cars, European beer, European food, tourists, travel, learning a language, the Champions League, the Ryder Cup, ABBA, Juliette Binoche, Sauvignon Blanc or even driving on the other side of the road.

They don't even object particularly to half a million Poles coming here to work as long as they are better than most of the work-shy incompetents that we currently have to consider for employment.

No, what really annoys COBs about Europe is that while every other country in the EU has a referendum every second month on whether pork sausages are better than beef, we were asked back in 1975 whether we thought Europe was a good idea (after we had already joined) and have never been asked anything since – while important decisions on expansion, trade, justice, agriculture, fishing, currency, the metric system and cheese are made far away by Peter Mandleson et al.

This also explains why no government will ever hold a referendum again on Europe in this country and expect to win, as every single COB has stored up 30 years of bitterness at being ignored and will vote NO to whatever question they are asked.

EUROVISION SONG CONTEST

Oh Lordi. What can you say about 50 years of European integration, cooperation, love and understanding that end up with 'Hard Rock Hallelujah'? Now if they had amalgamated Eurovision with Jeux Sans Frontieres and had performers singing whilst dressed as pandas on ice collecting water, that might be worth sitting through several hours of voting for.

F

FAIRNESS

Life is not fair. If it was, Jimmy White would have won the World Snooker Championship and Patrick Kielty would be out of work.

FAMILIES

Can't live with them. Can't change your DNA. Depressing really.

FAMOUS BRITONS

When, in 2000, the BBC ran a nationwide poll of 100 Greatest Britons, thousands voted in. The final top ten were all English, were all dead and were all famous in their own field. But how do they rank for crabbitness?

Elizabeth 1

Or, as Scottish COBs point out, Elizabeth of England, as she never ruled Scotland despite chopping off Mary Queen of Scots' head.

Elizabeth was one of a long line of Britons who were or are strong, iconic, humourless women. Victoria, Margaret Thatcher and Jordan all fit this stereotype. Elizabeth reigned for 40 years, saw off the Spaniards, ruled over a period of political stability and economic prosperity and was astute, pragmatic and ruthless.

COB rating: High. For all recent television attempts to turn Queen Bess into a foxy redhead, Elizabeth was a tough old boot, married to her job and her country rather than any Leicester or Essex and not averse to a little execution when roused.

William Shakespeare

The world's favourite playwright, who is still so omnipresent 400 years after his death that you would think that somebody else would have written some plays in the meantime. Without Shakespeare, a considerable amount of pubs in Britain would have no name, *Late Review* would only last 15 minutes every week and what would Kenneth Brannagh do for a living?

Not that COBs have seen a Shakespeare play since school. Not much point really as they usually all die in the end. Which is much the same reason COBs gave for not spending four hours watching *Titanic* when they know the boat is going to sink.

COB rating: High. Fair enough he wrote comedies, but the gags are not exactly Morecambe and Wise. And it is the cheery tragedies of King Lear, Othello, Macbeth *and* Hamlet *that he is best known for, with special mention for the sheer feel-good factor of the ending of* Romeo and Juliet *which will really set you up for a fun weekend.*

Oliver Cromwell

The republicans' republican who achieved the ultimate goal of overthrowing the monarchy. Organised, sincere, militarily adept, ruthless, puritan, guilty of regicide and reviled in Ireland, Cromwell has an ambivalent place in British history. Both democrat and dictator, man of God and man of war, anti-monarchists let him off for being on the right side and the middle classes let him off by calling their sons Oliver.

COB rating: Exceptionally high. 99.9% of all COBs would instinctively be a Roundhead rather than a Cavalier. All sides would agree that Cromwell was not a bundle of laughs, but to be fair the banning of Morris dancing can only be considered a good thing.

Isaac Newton

Eminent scientist. Discovered that if you drop an apple from a reasonable height it doesn't taste too good. That there are only seven true colours in the world and none of them are beige. And that calculus is a form of maths that you never need to know again after the age of 18.

COBs have mixed feelings about scientists. On the one hand they find it appalling that the youth of today eschew physics and chemistry for the insular pointlessness of marketing and media studies, on the other hand most scientists are clearly potentially mad and left to their own devices would take over the world.

It is not that COBs are against progress and change. Life before power showers was a bleak world indeed. However, COBs have an innate suspicion that once you get used to one change then some scientist invents something else. iPods and MP3 players for example – what was so wrong with cassettes and listening to the wireless?

COB rating : High. As obsessively ambitious mad scientists go Newton was well up there. Interested in alchemy, his later years were spent trying to invent real golden delicious apples.

Horatio Nelson

Sailor, admiral, victor at Trafalgar, Nelson stood against the might of Napoleon and the introduction into Britain of decent food.

For centuries Britain ruled the waves due to the strength of their navy and their fondness for rum, sodomy and the lash – or if you prefer drinking, homosexuality and corporal punishment. Nelson was the most famous of Britain's seafarers, dying in his finest hour and commemorated by being stuck on a plinth in the middle of lots of pigeons.

COB rating: Moderate. On the one hand, a brave commander who led his fleet to decisive victories around the world despite losing an eye, an arm and having to wear ever more ridiculous hats. On the other hand, a romantic who fell in love with both Lady Hamilton and, before he made his name in Hollywood, Oliver Hardy.

Isambard Kingdom Brunel

Engineer. Builder of railways, civic buildings, bridges and ships. And not any old ships, but, with the *Great Britain* and the *Great Eastern*, the largest ships the world had ever seen.

COBs as a rule do not mind travelling on trains as

long as they run on time and there are no screaming children or drunks or screaming drunken children in their carriage. If only they'd do away with those ridiculous untrustworthy automatic toilets that you are never sure if they going to expose you to the entire world and if only they did not charge you £3 for a teabag, tepid water and a Kit Kat then rail travel might be approaching enjoyable.

Interestingly, the world of architecture and project management that Brunel had to deal with is similar to that of today, with projects and buildings overspending, being mired in controversy and prone to excessive delays. Both New Wembley and the Scottish Parliament have the feel of a Brunel project, although one must imagine that he would have done better than the overblown 1970s local council offices that Holyrood in Edinburgh has ended up as.

COB rating: Low. Brunel was too much of a maverick and a dreamer. Always designing, always inventing and always short of money. He invented ocean liners and is therefore responsible for the career of Jane MacDonald. And with his whiskers, top hat and cigar he was sartorially so far ahead of his time that 150 years later his style has yet to come into fashion.

Charles Darwin

The Darwinian period of history that we currently live in may through natural selection prove to be relatively short. Either the evangelical right of America will turn the world creationist by bombing everybody who doesn't agree with them or global warming and the destruction of the ozone layer will end the whole debate on evolution as there will soon be nothing left on earth to evolve from.

COBs as a rule are strong supporters of Darwin and evolution as it supports their superiority complex. Of course you will also find COBs who will disagree with evolution just to be awkward.

COB rating: High. For all the excitement and adventures with giant turtles in his youthful travails around the globe in the Beagle, *Darwin spent the rest of his life obsessively studying and espousing his findings and growing a beard of Ayatollah-ish proportions. Although, as we have always said – if you are going to change the world in which you live in the face of universal derision, then you need a bit of the COB about you.*

Winston Churchill

Britain's second favourite Prime Minister of all time after Clement Attlee was a man who was captured in the Boer War, was sacked for the insanity that was the Gallipolli campaign in the First World War, was voted out of Parliament by the good folk of Dundee, failed to become the leader of the Conservatives, the Liberals and any other party he happened to be a member of and still came back for more.

When you think of Britain in the Second World War and the eventual defeat of fascism, the voice and face you think of is Arthur Lowe as Captain Mainwaring, but after him it is that of Winston Churchill.

COB rating: Moderate. Yes, he was an MP until 90 and Prime Minister until 80 and yes he was stubborn and irascible. But Churchill was too controversial, too unpredictable, too inspiring a speaker and drank too much brandy to be truly a great COB.

John Lennon

In this day and age when Guns N' Roses, Kate Bush and The Blue Nile can take over 10 years to make an album, it is remarkable to think that the entire recording career of the Beatles with 24 number one singles and 11 number one albums in the UK and the US, and probably the most important songbooks of the 20th century, all took place in just seven years. As well as music, The Beatles invented long hair, sideburns, short skirts, the pill, sex before marriage, drugs before marriage, if you were lucky sex and drugs after marriage, satire, colour television and the curious idea that all Liverpudlians are humorous.

They split up in 1970 and none of them were as good again, except Ringo who went on to do the voice of Thomas the Tank Engine. Even 'Imagine' is overplayed and somewhat of a dirge – as are all the various attempts by Oasis to cover it.

There was lots of truly dreadful music in the sixties – Cliff, Cilla, Engelbert, Tom Jones etc – but the good stuff (and the Beatles were good) still brings a proud tear to the eye of the most crabbit of COBs of a certain age. As long as they don't go and reform 40 years on – which is just plain sad.

COB rating: Potentially high. Tragically we will never know the full extent of John's cobbiness, but as Paul, Ringo and the late George have as multi-millionaires and living legends go, not exactly been rays of sunshine in recent years and as John had always been the most acerbic and stroppy of the four – then if he had lived he may have become the greatest COB of all time.

Princess Diana

Or Lady Diana, or the Queen of Hearts. The woman who made blonde the hair colour of choice for an entire generation. The woman who, with her ex-husband, did everything in her power to bring down the royal family. The woman who extended the career of Phil Collins and Dire Straits for far longer than was necessary.

When Diana died in 1997, the entire nation plunged into weeks of national mourning, mass hysteria and buying Elton John records. The entire nation, that is, except for the numerous COBs who, whilst feeling sorry for her children, could not see farther than a disturbed Sloane searching for the most unsuitable billionaire she could find. There were hundreds of complaints when the BBC cancelled *Antiques Roadshow* the day after – all of them from COBs.

COB rating: Low. Died too young and too flighty to be a COB. If she had lived she had the potential to succeed Joan Collins as British Queen of Hollywood. Victoria Beckham is the latest pretender to Ms Collins' throne, but is clearly not posh enough.

FASHION

Beep-beep, as David Bowie once said. Which must be similar to the thoughts flashing through the minds of those reluctant mild-mannered women having their breasts squeezed by Trinny and Susannah in *What Not To Wear*. COBs of course would never appear with Trinny and Susannah, not least because, as with Ant and Dec and Dick and Dom, they have no idea which one is which.

COBs' whole philosophy as regards fashion is either to ignore it altogether or to have enjoyed 1984 so much that they continue to dress as if Wham never split up.

In particular COBs hate shopping for clothes with a loathing rarely matched by anything else in this book. The queues, the music, the parking, the crowds, the remembering of PIN numbers, the disaffected, unsmiling staff with the unnecessary displaying of excess stomachs (is that really supposed to make you buy something when the assistant cannot wear something that fits?) and the constant threat of accidentally finding oneself lingering in the lingerie department, all have to be overcome even before you get to said trying of garments and the sheer joy of the changing room.

Will they have the right size?

If they have the right size is it actually the size it claims to be?

And if the right size is the right size then am I still the right size?

What size am I anyway?

Then there's the pricing. If one item is £5 and a not dissimilar item is £50 – how much are you supposed to pay? One's too expensive and one is going to fall apart, but which is which?

The only solution is for someone (not your mother) to buy something half-decent for you that more or less fits and to then be inordinately grateful. If you're lucky they might just buy all the rest of your clothes for you. Alternatively, stick to denim.

FANCIES

COBs are partial to a fancy or two. Lemon slice, almond slice, vanilla slice, cherry bakewell, angel cake, fairy cake and rock cake are all some of the many favourites that have made coffee mornings and afternoon teas slightly more bearable, although heaven help you if you use too much butter in the baking. There is however a fancy too far – the sickly sweet marzipan overload that is Battenburg. Of which the phrase have your cake and eat it only applies to people over the age of 85.

FISHING

COBs are keen to go fishing when they get the opportunity. The solitude, the concentration, the waders, the disillusionment and regret for opportunities lost and the eternal struggle for supremacy between man and trout. The main drawback being that COBs don't really like fish much.

FOOTBALL

Of all the major sports in the world, it is the Beautiful Game that appears most populated with COBs. From what seems like forever, dour, coat-wearing, dictatorial, mostly Scottish managers such as Stein, Busby, Shankly, Ferguson and Jim McLean have dominated British football without ever once being known to break into a smile.

Further COBs appear in the form of ex-players and sacked managers who proliferate on television and radio as analysts and pundits. They consistently fail to hide their bitterness at no longer having a job as a manager and being forced to watch overpaid, overindulged, under-performing players who earn ten times as much in a year as they did in their entire career.

To be fair to COBs, the modern game is over-exposed, often mediocre and increasingly uncompetitive with excessive wealth in the hands of a select few and with only one truly great player and one decent World Cup every decade. All this nostalgia, however, for the days of crumbling toilets in stadiums, hooligans in and out of the grounds, incessant kicking of anybody half-decent by brutal defenders with scary sideburns, incessant back passing to the goalkeeper, institutional racism, the annual excitement of the Wales v Northern Ireland home international and Coventry City's away strip is just taking things too far.

INTERNATIONAL FOOTBALL

International football and tournaments such as the World Cup bring out the true COB. Scratch the surface and all sorts of intolerance and cliché become apparent. The diving, cheating South Americans, the clinical Germans, the arrogant Dutch, the cynical Italians, the plucky but naive Africans, the samba-loving, bikini-wearing Brazilians who all play on the Copacabana beach and, 20 years after the fall of the Berlin Wall, we still get those dour, monochrome East Europeans.

Even worse for COBs is that they too get sucked

in by the excitement of the World Cup. They get their wallcharts, watch every game they can (and the evening highlights as well) and truly believe that this might be the year that Spain actually do something. Then, as the knockout rounds begin, the stark reality of modern football becomes clear – defensive attrition with only one forward per team, systematic diving and negative coaches playing for penalties. Not so much the Beautiful Game, more a soul-destroying reaffirmation that all that matters in life is whether your defensive midfielder protecting the back four is better than everybody else's.

Where English and Scottish COBs are concerned the stakes are even higher. The English inexplicably – given their propensity for their bottle to crash over the last 40 years – work themselves into a state of feverish anticipation every tournament. They also work themselves into a state of paranoia about why the Scots/Welsh/Irish will support every single one of their opponents rather than support them.

Scottish COBs on the other hand work themselves into tortuous indignation about some misjudged slip by an English commentator back in 1982 or try and rationalise their support for Portugal by the fact that their aunt and uncle had a nice holiday in the Algarve to deflect their anti-Englishness. Scottish COBs (some of whom were not even born in 1966) become even more combustible at the mere mention of a certain match between England and Germany and (much like the fact that more Scots fought against rather than for the Jacobites at Culloden) would much prefer that this was never referred to again.

FRANCE

COBs have a sneaking respect for the French. They may be arrogant buggers who keep losing wars, have rubbish music, make wilfully pretentious movies and elect Jacques Chirac, but on the other hand their obsession with protecting French language and culture, their militant farmers and lorry-drivers, their insistence on shops only selling one specific item, their cheese, their wine, their wilfully pretentious movies (could they not be bothered giving *Hidden* a half-decent ending?), their determination to smoke super-strength cigarettes whenever possible and their willingness to say *merde* to the Americans are all, when you think of it, traits that COBs can do nothing else but admire.

FREEDOM

The right to say, do, eat, drink, drive, smoke, basically whatever you want as long as you are not hurting anybody else. Instead of being told what to do, when you can do it and having every waking moment legislated for and filmed on CCTV – with ID cards and electronic chips inserted at birth to follow. No longer is it enough for you to know who you are, everybody else has to know as well.

G

GAMBLING

COBs are not life's natural gamblers. There is the moral dilemma that you should only get out of life what you put into it and the logical dilemma of spending hard-earned cash on what is basically chance. But what really puts COBs off gambling is the possibility of not winning. They may have successfully predicted the last five Derby winners, the winner of the World Cup and what round Andy Murray will get knocked out at Wimbledon, but when they do actually have a modest flutter, not only is watching the event in question ruined by the tension of having a whole £5 riding on it, the desolation of losing is almost too much to bear.

This is why *Deal Or No Deal* never have COBs on the show as COBs would always accept the Banker's first offer after five minutes of the show – never mind how much Noel witters on about cosmic ordering.

GOLF

COBs like a round of golf. The lifelong journey around the same eighteen portions of grass with attached sand and water in the vain search of that perfect round where you take less than three putts per hole and end up with a net gain of golf balls.

COB golfers will play in rain, wind, sleet and will consider snow. They do not wear yellow, pink, or beige golfwear. They think that Colin Montgomerie is deep down a big girl's blouse and, on the very rare occasions that they play matchplay, never ever concede a single putt and always presume that their opponent is a cheating bandit.

GREETINGS CARDS

Of all the many retail emporiums that COBs never set foot in, greetings card shops are probably the ones they avoid the most.

The only birthday they remember is their own and they don't see getting older as something to celebrate. Christmas is excessively commercial and the wife deals with it anyway. Even if parents are alive, Mother's and Father's Day simply don't register and, as for Valentine's Day, the best you can expect is the annual washing of the dishes.

H

HARRY POTTER

COBs have never read a whole Harry Potter book, but have managed to just about sit through one of the movies to see what all the fuss was about, although afterwards were still none the wiser. Robbie Coltrane wandering around with a big beard being all that they remembered.

COBs are impressed though by the sheer size of these inexplicable bestsellers. The longer that they keep children occupied the better.

HATS

Both male and female COBs have a propensity for hats or caps or bonnets. This is not, as you might first think, a response to ongoing hair loss as COBs on average are more hirsute than non-COBs, but more a practical step at an early age to avoid the danger of intermittent rainfall which over the years has become such an item of faith that no journey outdoors (or even indoors for that matter) can be contemplated without trusty hat safely attached to head, impervious to heatwave or force nine gales.

HEALTH

Whilst the rest of the population spend their time suffering with sniffs, aches, pains, stress and nausea, COBs proudly rise above such grumblings. Little short of limb amputation would get them near a doctor and it would take a plague of bubonic proportions to miss a day at work.

Not that COBs do not have strong opinions on health. Deeply suspicious of people phoning in sick, nothing riles more than a minor cold being described as dying with the flu. Stress and depression are other ailments which do not impress COBs – life is not meant to be enjoyable so just get on with it. And as for therapists and psychoanalysts, fair play to them for charging hundreds of pounds for listening and nodding while people prattle on about how nobody understands them, but you do think the poor sods would realise that if listening and nodding is what they need then a dog would be a lot cheaper.

On the positive side, COBs are strong believers in a bath being a cure for all known ailments from aches and strains to bird flu. However, they do not hold with any of that aromatherapy candle nonsense, which are not only pungent but clearly potential fire hazards.

HEATING

If is often thought that COBs have an amazing tolerance against the cold, as this must be the only reason to explain why fires are never put on and central heating is only switched on when the next ice age is imminent. COBs can also be said to have been at the forefront of domestic environmentalism, as for years they have been switching off all household appliances long before it was fashionable to do so.

HOLY GRAIL

Now, COBs like nothing more than a good thriller or an interesting conspiracy theory – and while *The Da Vinci Code* was neither, it did make a change from the usual diet of American serial killers and gruesome forensic examiners and the hundreds of books with either death, blood or bones in the title. But one book about Jesus liking the ladies every decade or so is plenty and we can do without all the follow-ups of serial killer knights/monks searching for lost earthenware Habitat cups in the deepest Pyrenees.

However, if a descendant of Jesus had assassinated JFK before being abducted by aliens and then returning as Diana's love child – now that might be worth reading.

HOUSE OF LORDS

It is always ironic when a government cites freedom and democracy as their motives for international action and not only have an unelected second chamber, but an unelected second chamber that you may or may not get into by paying large amounts of money. Not that there is anything intrinsically wrong with politicians making a bit of cash, but do they have to be quite as unsubtle about it? Multiple properties, offshore trusts, directorships, several Jaguars etc do not really sit well with the men-and-women-of-the-common-people look.

HUNTING

COBs have no time for mindless cruelty, whether it be poisoning badgers, stealing rare bird's eggs, upper class buffoons charging around the countryside trying to rip a fox apart or evil little brats shooting pets with air rifles. However they have no problem with a bit of judicious hunting on the basis of keeping numbers down or protecting livestock and would happily consider culling pigeons and seagulls in cities or gangs of hooded youths for the greater good.

I

ITV

COBs always historically prefer the BBC to the more populist, more working class, more downmarket ITV. *Blue Peter*, *Swap Shop* and *The Good Life* viewers rather than *Magpie*, *Tiswas* and *Mind Your Language*. COBs will claim that, while most TV is rubbish these days, ITV is just one big diet of Ant and Dec, soap operas and instantly forgettable dramas starring one of Martin Kemp, Ross Kemp or Tasmin Outhwaite-Kemp.

However the real reason COBs don't watch ITV is that they can't bear all the adverts. You are watching a film and, after every fifteen minutes, you get five minutes of adverts, and after an hour of that, you then get half an hour of news, five minutes of local news (almost always centred around some grim housing estate or other) and then interminable weather. How anyone can sit through all of that and still keep watching is beyond comprehension. No wonder ITV lose millions of viewers every year.

IRELAND

Ah the Irish, the Celtic Tiger, the land of myths and legends, of Finn MacCool and leprechauns. The land of Guinness and Murphy's, where the craic is mighty, the music never stops, the whiskey always flows, good food is only a spud away and the confident talking of bollocks is never-ending.

Ah Ireland, the land of Yeats, Wilde, Joyce, Becket, Behan, Shane MacGowan, Roy Keane and Brian O'Driscoll. And the land of Adams, McGuinness, Paisley, Dana, Eamonn Holmes, U2, Bob Geldof, Daniel O'Donnell and bloody Patrick Kielty. God, COBs cannot be doing with Ireland.

J

JAZZ

COBs are the only remaining people in the world who can tolerate jazz. While the rest of the population run screaming from the mere prospect of a few minutes of Thelonius Monk or Oscar Peterson COB jazz aficionados will think nothing of listening to John Coltrane failing to locate any recognisable tune or melody for hours on end.

JOKES

Jokes are not COBs' strong points. They only know four jokes, don't understand three of them and tend to forget what the punchline is to all of them.

Joke 1: They have difficulties comprehending the inherent dangers of a chicken crossing the road.

Joke 2: They always forget what animal a man walks into a bar with and usually end up with a giraffe having a long face.

Joke 3: They do remember that the panda eats, shoots and leaves, but are somewhat disturbed by the bestiality angle and the lack of bamboo in the joke.

Joke 4: 'Who Fired That Cannon?' is, by a process of elimination, the COBs' favourite joke of all-time. Although they never remember how it goes and always mess up the punchline.

K

KETTLES

Of all household implements, COBs would find it most difficult if they were forced to do without their kettle. Whether it be tea or coffee, and it is always one or the other, they drink gallons of the stuff. But not just any old tea or coffee. Oh no.

Tea or coffee must be drunk in one specific cup or mug (which nobody else can ever use), with the same amount of milk, sugar, both, or neither, every time – and heaven help you if you forget to put the milk in first or take the teabag out in less than thirty seconds.

As for Earl Grey, camomile and any of the other plethora of herbal, fruit, flavoured and organic variations that are available, COBs would rather drink cider and blackcurrant through a straw.

L

LANGUAGE

It is often thought that people who are crabbit are not great talkers. Men and women of few words – monosyllabic or giving only the odd humphff to acknowledge the fact that someone has spoken to them and a response is called for.

Whilst it is certainly true that you do meet COBs who consider conversation a dangerous pastime on a par with ten-pin bowling, you also meet many other COBs who can drone on for hours about whatever subject happens to be exercising them on that given day.

These subjects can be as diverse as a footballer's metatarsal, where you get the best tasting strawberries, the next door neighbour's romantic predilections or the almost inevitable discussion on the merits of European integration.

The key to talkative COBs is that whatever the topic the important thing to remember is that, no matter what, no credit can be given at any time whatsoever. To COBs, food should always taste better, governments can always govern better, sportsmen can always play better, everything can cost less and all good deeds have a hidden agenda.

The following phrases are all ones that no self-respecting COB will ever be heard to utter:

Never mind, everybody did their best.
It's done now, so let's look to the future.
That was worth every penny.
What the hell, let's go for the five star hotel.
Wasn't that a wise decision by the courts?
All this immigration is certainly making us a more vibrant, exciting society.
Look no further, it was all my fault.
I'll cook tonight, darling.
Wouldn't it be nice if Mr Blair stayed on for another nine years?
That colour really suits you.

LANGUAGES (FOREIGN)

COBs are very much in favour of learning languages. Children should be educated to speak properly and clearly, and all tourists, visitors and immigrants should speak good English so that they can be understood at all times. The only drawback to this love of linguistics is travelling abroad. Whilst in an ideal world it would be preferable to diligently study the phrase books and listen to the language tapes, COBs are of the opinion that actually speaking a foreign language would be counter-productive as either:

1) They will reply in perfect English anyway
2) They will reply and you won't catch a word of it

Therefore always best to stick to Plan A of talking very slowly and pointing.

LIBERAL DEMOCRATS

The Liberal Democrats – where did it all go wrong? There they were minding their own business, keeping quiet and with a leader who believed in doing as little as possible – and in return they had their biggest number of MPs and share of the vote for 80 years, gaining supporters from both Labour and the Tories, and with future success, coalition government and proportional representation all within their grasp. And what do they go and do? Start taking themselves seriously, having policy initiatives all over the place, demanding that their leaders are sober at all times and electing the poshest grandad that they could find. Not that COBs ever voted Lib Dem anyway – far too liberal for them.

LIFE EXPECTANCY

As you would imagine by their middle name, COBs tend to live to and beyond the average life expectancy of people in Britain. In Glasgow, where life expectancy is seven years less than the rest of Britain, the onset of crabbitness, in order to be consistent, begins much earlier.

On the one hand, it seems cruel to prolong the misery, irritation and disappointment that COBs have to put up with by expecting them to live to such excessive longevity, but on the other, these extra years give COBs an opportunity to hone their crabbitness to even greater heights of louder tutting and more pronounced shaking of heads. And it's a chance to experience even more of the unspeakable developments in modern life which COBs like to go on about for hours on end.

JENNIFER LOPEZ

If you ask most COBs who or what J-Lo is, most wouldn't know and a minority would plump for some new-fangled fruit drink. Other Americans that COBs don't know include Eminem, 50 Cent, Paris Hilton, Chris Rock and Christina Aguilera. They do, however, know that R Kelly is that strange cabinet minister with the eyebrows and disconcertingly deep voice.

Reassuringly, COBs are as partial to a nice arse as everybody else.

LUNCH

Where did all this lunch come from? You used to know where you were with meals. Breakfast, dinner, tea and supper, all at the appropriate times. Tea was never later than 6.30 and lunch was reserved for Sundays and usually involved lashings of gravy. Now dinner is anytime before midnight and lunch is a £3 pack of sandwiches which may or may not contain pickle.

M

GILLIAN McKEITH

When we are talking of COBs of an especially Scottish hue, we eventually end up with Dr Gillian McKeith. Who, to paraphrase the old joke, if her TV programme is called *You Are What You Eat*, must be devouring especially bitter wasps on a regular basis.

It is, of course, a good thing to promote healthy eating and nutrition and highlight the dangers of obesity. It is also true that the poor fat fools who appear on these reality car crash programmes have voluntarily agreed and thoroughly deserve their fifteen minutes of fame and public humiliation. It therefore would take a COB of extraordinary crabbitness to engender empathy with every single victim (no matter how stupid) and create in the viewer the desire to consume as many crisps, packets of biscuits and gallons of lager as humanly possible. Dr Gillian McKeith is said COB.

MAGAZINES

There are many things to be irritated by at railway and airport shops. Why are bottles of water more expensive that Coke? And who in their right mind wants to buy a half-price metric ton of chocolate with their *Daily Telegraph*? What is absolutely bewildering however is the plethora of identical magazines with the same five women on the cover, who are apparently either too fat, too skinny, heartbroken, pregnant or considering becoming even more unfeasibly top-heavy.

Now it is one thing trying to work out what exactly are the point of these women and what was so wrong with *Woman's Own* and their features on At Home With Hannah Gordon but, more importantly, why do you need so many magazines to tell you the same story 'KERRY BREAKS NAIL TRAUMA – ICELAND HEARTBREAK'? And even more importantly – where's my free bag?

MAGIC

COBs take the biblical line as far as magic is concerned. Turning water into wine, healing the sick, raising the dead and parting large volumes of water can all be considered worthwhile and useful exercises.

But as for finding the five of spades in your pocket or a 10p behind your ear, making a piece of rope stand up straight or finding a rabbit in a hat – what exactly is the point? Unless you actually know somebody who would like a rabbit. And as for sawing a lady in half – surely that is illegal in most countries of the world.

MARRIAGE

Much like horses and electric fences, COBs and weddings do not really go together. All those family members forced together in one place with no opportunity of escape. The airing of the ten-year-old suit (if the moths haven't got there first) or the sheer hell of having to buy a new outfit when nothing in the wardrobe appears to fit anymore. The tedium of the speeches where the only clue that a joke has been attempted is when the words 'But on a serious note' are uttered. The interminable waiting for the food to finally arrive and the evening long strategy of avoiding at all costs being made to dance to 'Is This The Way To Amarillo'.

A survey by the *You And Your Wedding* magazine worked out that the cost of an average wedding is now £20k. Average cost of a wedding organised by COBs however is £405 and grudgingly at that.

Male COBs are generally not asked on stag nights. Female COBs do however get asked on hen parties mainly for the amusement of seeing them wear pink cowboy hats and 'GIRLS ON TOUR' T-shirts.

MASTERMIND

COBs like a good quiz, as long as the questions are not too easy and they don't lose. COBs do not like losing.

Their favourite TV show used to be *Mastermind* which had a black chair, a grey Icelander and serious questions on subjects such as the naval stratagems of Horatio Nelson and the architecture of the Hittites. They are not so sure about the all-new *Mastermind* with John Humphrys. Not only do they allow questions on specialist subjects such as *The Simpsons* and Atomic Kitten, but they also have an excruciating middle part where Humphrys attempts Chris Tarrant-esque bonhomie with contestants who just wish he would shut up and ask them who the Greek god of dove-racing is.

At least *Mastermind* is immeasurably better than your standard GMTV quiz:

Question: What is the capital of France?
A) Paris

B) Harris

C) Princess Michael of Kent

MATHEMATICS

COBs are strong proponents of the three R's of reading, writing and arithmetic. Although the very fact that one of the three R's begins with an A annoys them. As far as COBs are concerned there is nothing more infuriating than watching a contestant on *The Weakest Link* or a similar show looking vacantly at the quizmaster with no possibility of their brain being able to understand the concept of what is seven times eight.

COBs themselves are great fans of all sorts of letter and number puzzles from crosswords to wordsearches to the Rubik's Cube and the modern craze of Su Doku, and believe inherently that these puzzles have the power to hold back senility. The more difficult the puzzle the better as far as COBs are concerned. Little can match the smug satisfaction on completion, or the almost suicidal desolation after six hours of intense concentration when you end up with two sixes in the last column of Super Su Doku.

MEDICAL ADVANCES

Whilst the rest of us are impressed by the amazing advances in medical science such as keyhole surgery, DNA identification, hearts, kidney, liver and even face transplants, COBs are suspicious about whose heart, kidney, liver etc you might end up with. For heaven's sake, you might end up with a *Daily Star* reader keeping you going.

MID-LIFE CRISIS

For many people the years from 35 to 45 are prone to serious concerns about life, relationships, children, health and employment. This can manifest itself in excessive wearing of Ben Sherman shirts and GAP jeans, the purchasing of albums by heavily hyped indie bands, the taking-up of jogging and badminton and socialising with colleagues fifteen years younger than oneself.

COBs also suffer from mid-life crises, but usually much earlier – around the age of 23 – and focusing on the key COB question of whether to grow a beard or a moustache and what percentage of one's salary one should put into a pension.

MOBILE PHONES

Less than 1 out of 5 adults in Britain do not own a mobile phone. Almost all of these people are COBs who really cannot stand the things. Whether it's being made to listen other peoples inane conversations on trains and buses, seeing drivers chatting away when they should be concentrating on the road or being startled by grown men and women talking loudly to themselves as they walk along the street with pieces of wire sticking out of their ears, there is no excuse for 99% of mobile phone calls.

COBs simply cannot understand people's utter dependence on the mobile – how on earth did these people survive before its invention? When you made arrangements and stuck to them, when you phoned your mum on a Sunday evening, you did not feel the need to tell the entire world that you were in the supermarket and you actually made the effort to talk to the people you were in the company of rather than texting gibberish to somebody else.

MONEY

COBs sincerely believe that money is the root of all evil. Usually this is because they don't have any money in the first place or, if they do have money, the process of spending it is just too painful to endure.

MOVIES

Now, no matter how bad Hollywood movies are these days, and boy are most of them bad, nothing can quite match the sheer awfulness of modern British movies – whether it be excruciatingly bad gangster movies (with or without Vinnie Jones), mediocre comedies with TV stars way out of their depth, or anything with either John Hannah or Richard E. Grant in it. The cinematic equivalent of hell would be a British remake of *Some Like It Hot* set in Torquay and starring Billie Piper or Cat Deeley as Sugar and both John Hannah and Richard E. Grant in drag in a final stand-off to decide once and for all who is the worst actor of all-time.

MUSIC

Just because COBs don't dance does not mean that they don't like music. Quite the reverse. Another early sign of crabbitness is an obsessive interest in music at a young age combined with alphabetically cataloguing one's record collection and never lending records to anyone – especially younger sisters. It is also at this early stage that COBs will discover their musical favourites – whether it be Caruso, Beethoven, Sinatra, Johnny Cash, the Beatles, Morrissey or Gary Numan – who they like so much that there is absolutely no point listening to anybody else.

COBs are especially devoted to Elvis (Presley rather than Costello). As far as they are concerned nothing worth the cost of vinyl has been recorded since 1977 and the answer to life, the universe and everything can be found in the lyrics of 'In The Ghetto'.

MUSICALS

Inexplicably popular entertainment for those who like neither good theatre nor good music, but like to go out of an evening and feel bingo is beneath them.

It is perhaps unfair to dismiss an entire genre so cavalierly. Without musicals, the careers of Tommy Steele, Michael Flatley and Darren Day may never have happened and musicals have given numerous former pop and soap stars an alternative to working in Tescos. However, has anybody ever met someone who can sing-a-long-a *Miss Saigon*?

N

NATIONAL HEALTH SERVICE

The bottomless financial pit that is the pride and joy of Britain's Welfare State, which no COB will ever say a good word about no matter how good the treatment they receive. The irony of this is that for all that COBs either avoid the NHS as much as possible or incessantly moan about doctors, consultants and GPs, nothing riles them more than the prospect of privatisation or closing down local hospitals and moving them five miles out of town next to your B&Q Superstore so that you can buy some magenta gloss finish while you wait to get stitches put in. More to the point, when any political party announces that the NHS is safe in their hands, ever-suspicious COBs will always automatically not believe them and vote for the other lot.

NATIONAL LOTTERY

COBs cannot abide the National Lottery. A stealth tax on the lower classes to fund the opera and the

Olympics or another state sponsored scheme to increase gambling and personal debt are probably the more measured comments that they have on the subject.

However, this does not stop them from faithfully spending their £1 a week and even tolerating bloody Eamonn Holmes to find out every Saturday that once again their lives have not changed one iota.

NATURAL HISTORY

COBs like natural history programmes. From *World About Us* and *Survival* to the numerous BBC series of David Attenborough breathlessly criss-crossing the globe, you cannot beat a good bit of footage of cheetahs chasing an unfortunate gazelle in slow motion and penguins falling over on an ice floe.

This in turn explains COBs antipathy to zoos. All very well keeping species alive, but it just doesn't seem right seeing a seriously pissed off tiger wandering around a compound in the West Midlands or a clinically depressed polar bear on a summer's day in Surrey. Zoos are also full of groups of kids attempting but unfortunately failing to fall into the enclosures. Ghastly places.

NEWSPAPERS

COBs like their daily newspaper. It forms part of their daily routine, along with the obligatory number of morning cups of tea or coffee and specific number of slices of toast. If any of these constants are but slightly wrong or, heaven forfend, missing, then the whole equilibrium of a COB's day is completely ruined.

This is another reason for COBs having difficulty travelling abroad. They can just about accept that the tea, coffee and toast might not be exactly as they have it at home, but the lack of a newspaper causes unmitigated distress which is only alleviated sometime in the afternoon when they finally track down a three-day-old copy of the international edition of the *Daily Express*.

NUCLEAR

COBs mourn the disappearance of CND from the news. They enjoyed nothing more than a vigorous discussion on the merits of possessing a nuclear deterrent which would inevitably conclude with the statement 'Go back to Russia then'.

As for nuclear power – just when you had been convinced that it was not safe, was too expensive and not good for your health, then the government changes its mind again and says nuclear power stations are the future, completely safe and ideal for primary school outings. A position which you might have a little more confidence in if they decided to build all the new reactors in Surrey.

O

OBITUARIES

As COBs get older they have an increasing interest in reading newspaper obituaries – specifically, a grim fascination on whether they are older or younger than the unfortunate deceased.

OPTICIANS

If 118 118 are unquestionably the worst adverts in the world and have ensured that millions of people will never ever use that service, then a runner-up must be the recent adverts from Dolland & Aitchison and their extremely disturbing contact lens wearing sausages.

Which brings us on to opticians and the not surprising fact that COBs are not frequent visitors to their stores. Not that COBs have better eyesight than everybody else but they will squint at signs, buy ever-larger TV screens and completely ignore acquaintances in the street rather than admit that they need glasses. And when finally, despite everything, there is no alternative and spectacles have to be purchased, these glasses will be kept for years and held together with rubber bands and sellotape rather than having to go back and endure another eye-test with some twenty-year-old breathing in your face from a distance of three inches, followed by having to choose from a selection of a hundred identical-looking pairs of glasses which you cannot see anyway.

P

PENSIONS

COBs spend a lot of time considering the whole question of pensions. An early sign of crabbitness is those 23-year-olds who have already put their retirement plans in place and religiously stick to the maximum pay-in level every month. An exciting Friday night for them is *River City* combined with a ham and pineapple pizza.

Whether it be company pensions, private pensions, ISAs, PEPs, insurance policies, life insurance policies or whatever new schemes are invented to confuse you even more, COBs have spent hundreds of hours investigating all the different options, reading all the literature, have met all the advisers and have saved and invested accordingly.

And once they have done all this, do they trust that pension companies will deliver what they promise, or that the government will provide an adequate state pension or believe that the annual £27 billion and counting pension deficit is going to get any better? Not in the slightest, and grimly expect nothing less than having to work in B&Q until at least the age of 80.

PERIOD DRAMA

COBs are not against historical dramas *per se*. Nothing wrong with a good war movie or naval drama or a classic western. To be accurate, as long as there is some combination of ships, planes, trains, tanks, guns and taciturn heroes doing what a taciturn hero has to do all is well with the world.

If *Pride and Prejudice* had Mr Darcy serving with Sharpe in the Napoelonic War and if *Wuthering Heights* had Heathcliff driving a jeep across the Yorkshire Moors then they would have been much improved. And by all means have a heaving bosom or two for a bit of scenery, but when it comes to romance – get a room somewhere so we can get on with the shootout at the vicarage.

THE POLICE

What has happened to today's police force? It is not just the often-repeated comment 'Don't they look younger these days?', but much more importantly haven't they become considerably shorter as well? In the old days you literally looked up to a policeman, but now you increasingly peer down at somebody five foot six or less.

Also, where have all the moustaches gone? How can you know and trust your bobby on the beat if there is no familiar and reassuring facial hair on the upper lip?

Finally, where have all the actors gone who can play taciturn, loner maverick detectives with relationship and alcohol issues who can single-handedly track down well-spoken serial killers, because Ken Stott must be absolutely knackered with all the different series he has to do. The only policeman role Ken Stott does not yet have is in Taggart, which itself has become increasingly unbelievable, not because Taggart died over ten years ago, but because it is a Glasgow crime series with such an unrealistically low murder count.

PORNOGRAPHY

Apparently there are 27 adult television channels available in the UK at the moment including Red Hot Movies, Red Hot Wives and Red Hot Rears. One imagines that unsuspecting gardening buffs might be somewhat taken aback by the content of Red Hot Pokers.

With so much to choose from, COBs so inclined

have a wide selection of channels to seek out the traditional COB merits of value for money, reliability and most importantly a good regular service.

PRINCE CHARLES

It is reassuring to see, in recent years, Prince Charles assume his father's role as chief royal COB. This accession was confirmed with his recent recommendation of cheery Canadian singer-songwriter Leonard Cohen and the sheer pleasure which must be St James Palace when Charles croons along to 'So Long Marianne', 'Sisters Of Mercy' and 'Suzanne Takes Me Down'. Which, at least as far as Camilla is concerned, makes a change from him banging on about architecture and organic farming.

PROPERTY

If Margaret Thatcher changed one thing above all others it was to create the mantra that all human happiness can be found in the buying and selling of property. COBs are as concerned about the property ladder and the importance of bricks and mortar as the next person, but once they have found their semi-detached castle of choice, they tend to raise the drawbridge and settle for life.

Although COBs have no interest in your *Changing Rooms*, *House Doctor*, *Grand Designs* and the gullible people who get excited by a pelmet or two, they will spend if not happy hours, then certainly hours and hours single-handedly putting in new doors, painting the garden fence, fiddling with the plumbing and endlessly driving back and forth from B&Q in the endless search for the perfect plank of wood.

'We will have to get a man in' is not a phrase ever uttered by any COB.

PUNISHMENT

COBs are in principle believers in the old eye for an eye, what goes around comes around and no smoke without fire view of crime and punishment. However, as their opinion of lawyers, the courts and Judge John Deed sleeping with both solicitors at once is not especially high, then on balance they can just about accept that we don't have capital punishment in this country as God knows how many unlucky unfortunates would get their necks stretched by mistake.

And that's before we get to the wisdom of the great British jury system and the will-we-reach-an-agreement-in-time-to-get-home-to-watch-the-football justice that they mete out. This is, clearly, only when there is not a COB on the jury doing their Henry Fonda duty by disagreeing with everybody else and painstakingly going through every piece of evidence for weeks on end.

Q

QUEUES

COBs hate queues. They will walk out of shops, walk out of bars, walk out of post offices, walk out of most everywhere if they have to wait more than five minutes.

COBs will set off on car, train and plane journeys hours in advance to try and avoid possible delays and having to queue.

In fact the only thing worse than queues are people who jump queues. VIPs, groups of six who have one person looking after the bags while the rest turn up thirty minutes later, and, finally, people (usually of limited stature) who vigorously use their elbows to gain inches at the queue for the bar whilst simultaneously shouting 'Two pints of Stella' in as obnoxious a way as possible in their obsessive determination to be served.

R

RABBITS

Fluffy little *Watership Down* Easter bunnies or insatiable crop-eating, countryside scarring vermin that are growing so big that the scary rabbit from *Donnie Darko* will soon become the future rather than just a nightmare. What do you think?

RACISM

Sad to say that many COBs are not strangers to racism and bigotry. Every nation, race and creed can be dismissed in a welter of Bernard Manning-esque stereotypes. The Scots, the English, the Welsh, the Irish, the French, the Germans, the Arabs, the Israelis, the Asians, the Japanese, the Americans etc etc, can all be interchanged with any of the following adjectives – mean, arrogant, drunken, ignorant, untrustworthy, strangers to soap and no oil paintings as far as COBs are concerned.

The only consolation to this misanthropic view of their fellow man and woman is that COBs can be as condemnatory of their fellow countrymen as any other poor sods – and you should hear them discussing their own family. The one exception to this derogatory overview is Scandinavians – COBs do shop in IKEA.

READING

COBs like to read. Whether it be crime thrillers, war stories, romantic sagas or histories of tanks of the world, they don't seem to mind that they are intrinsically reading the same book over and over again (can anyone actually tell one Patricia Cornwell novel from another?) and get especially annoyed when Maeve Binchy's latest is set in Iraq or when Ian Rankin gets carried away and tries to write a love scene.

REALITY TV

How many COBs watch Big Bother and how many COBs text in to vote Grace out on eviction night? Exactly the same number of people who watched more than one of Davina McCall's chat shows. 425.

RELIGION

COBs can either take or leave religion. If the slings and arrows of fortune have left one with some semblance of faith to sustain them to death and beyond – so be it. No logic or rationality is going to change things at this stage. By the same token COBs who are self-confessed atheists are almost evangelical in their faith of non-believing.

What all COBs tend to be united in is a complete dismissal of every religious faith other than their own. Thousands of years of history, philosophy, study, discourse, literature, architecture and art concerning the historic faiths of the world with billions of followers can be summed up as bible-bashing God-botherers, towel-heads and sandal-wearing hippies.

More COBs might go to Church if it wasn't for the compulsory singing. They can just about put up with the bizarre wearing of women's hats that even the Queen never made fashionable, but it is the rendition of hymns at a key that are two octaves too high and at a pitch that only cats finds comfortable that keep COBs walking the dog on a Sunday morning. As for clapping and guitars – just don't go there. COBs don't do Harlem.

RETAIL OFFERS

One of the many reasons COBs hate shopping is the irritation they feel at the numerous retail offers that are supposed to attract them to buy:

Buy One Get One Free
If I wanted two, I would buy two. What am I supposed to do with the second one?

Buy One Get One Half-Price
Yes I can see all the posters and all the stickers, but where does it tell you how much you actually have to pay?

Free plus postage and packing
So it's not free then?

99p
What's the difference between £9.99 and £10? Do they think I am that desperate for a bloody penny?

RHETORIC

There was Tommy Sheridan, Scottish Socialist Party MSP and that extremely rare specimen – a popular politician – in his finest hour on the steps of

Edinburgh High Court with his lovely wife Gail by his side, having taken on single-handedly his own political party and the full force of the Rupert Murdoch media empire and against all the odds been declared victorious. And what does he do in his moment of glory? He forgets rule number one of public speaking – that microphones actually amplify sound – and then rants some unintelligible nonsense about Gretna's football team beating Real Madrid on penalties (when in fact Gretna's football team are not very good at penalties). As far as COBs are concerned, listening to politicians speak is bad enough, but those that resort to roaring and raving in an Ian Paisley 'No surrender' stylee are people you wouldn't trust with running a bath, never mind running the country.

RHUBARB

COBs like rhubarb. They prefer rhubarb jam to strawberry jam and they prefer rhubarb crumble to apple crumble, preferably with ice cream rather than custard. There is no excuse for custard after the age of nine.

ROADWORKS

Always when traffic is busiest. Always with traffic lights that change every four months if at all. Sometimes with signs that say 'Take Windsor Street Diversion' – where the hell is Windsor Street? Always with men at work standing around looking quizzical. And when the men and the lights and the signs have all gone – what are you left with? Calming bumps that bugger your suspension. Calming – I'll give you bloody calming.

ROMANCE

To be honest, COBs struggle with courtship and wooing. Small matters such as expressing one's feelings, listening to someone else prattle on and disrupting one's tried and tested routines, are all issues that can prove difficult to overcome.

Partners of COBs tend to be infinitely patient and realistic people who will tolerate much for the greater good (no matter how unfathomable to the outside world that greater good may seem).

Once in a relationship COBs tend to mate for life. There are two reasons for this.

Firstly, COBs as a rule are determined people, so it is not unexpected that when they meet someone that they can actually put up with then they determine to doggedly pursue them and wear them down until they finally say yes.

Secondly, COBs are not without some self-awareness and realise that if some unsuspecting soul is brave or foolish enough to take them on, then as the old saying goes you don't look a gift-horse in the mouth – if for no other reason than you might get a dunt in the face.

To give a flavour of a romantic COB in action here are some of their best chat-up lines:

Now then

Looks like rain

It would be cheaper if we shared a taxi

You won't be wanting dinner will you

Just to let you know the last bus is at ten to ten

You're better looking than I first thought

That top is nice, did it cost much?

I've got an allotment

Once they have got used to their new routine and regular hot meals and have assimilated into coupledom, they are loathe to let anything or anyone disrupt this status quo. Adultery, although not unheard of, is unusual for COBs to partake of, as not only is flirting and chatting-up a somewhat alien concept for COBs to partake of, they can be so oblivious of others that little short of a stray hand in their nether regions is likely to grab their attention, so to speak.

ROYALTY

Some crabbit old buggers are keen supporters of the royal family. This is due to traditional patriotism, loyalty to the Queen and the uncomplaining dignity with which she has taken on the responsibility of wearing shocking yellow for over 50 years.

When pressed on their support for the royal family, COB monarchists will highlight the importance of royalty to the tourist industry – which somewhat ignores those well-known republican tourist destinations of France, Italy, Greece and the USA.

However, to be fair, the majority of COBs are fervent in their disapproval of our ruling family. Spoilt, inbred spongers who by quirk of birth have been given the right to squander millions of taxpayers' money is one of the milder COB opinions concerning the Windsors.

Ask a COB to express their thoughts on the warmth of Prince Philip, the humour of Princess Anne, the worth to society of Andrew and Edward, the moral authority and affinity with the common man of Charles and the general intelligence of the entire family and you will hear views that make you wonder what it takes to get charged with treason these days. The younger members of the royal family are usually excluded from such criticism on the grounds of their youth or until they start wearing Nazi uniforms.

On balance however, COBs are believers in patience rather than the firing squad option. If Charles doesn't single-handedly finish off the monarchy in this country when he finally gets the chance (no wonder his mother has no intention of abdicating) then one of his sons most certainly will.

ROLLING STONES

Many people think of the Rolling Stones as the ultimate COBs of rock and roll – 40 years of grumpy louche bad behaviour and 40 years of churning out 'I Can't Get No Satisfaction'. However when it comes to the ultimate COB supergroup of all time, no Stone makes it to the final selection:

Vocals: Van Morrison
Lead Guitar: Lou Reed
Rhythm Guitar: Chuck Berry
Bass: Roger Waters
Drums: Meg White (probably a bit harsh, but God does she look dour)
Keyboards: Nina Simone
Mouth Organ: Bob Dylan

Although to be honest the chances of all seven of them turning up at the same time at the same venue are fairly negligible.

RUSSIA

At least you know where you are with Russia. Once a freezing, glum, vodka-soaked, fur-wearing, dour, grumpy dictatorship, always a freezing, glum, vodka-soaked, fur-wearing, dour grumpy dictatorship. In other words Russians have all the qualities and attributes that COBs look for in a nation and always prefer to have the Bear with them than against them. As long as you never have to go there or attempt Cossack dancing – bad for your knees.

RUNNING

Taking up jogging is a common trait of thirty-somethings as an early sign of imminent mid-life crisis. Most people run for no more than five years before giving up to either save their crumbling knee joints, have an affair, drink three times the Ministry of Health's suggested limit, embrace their expanding stomach, play golf or all of the above.

However, running COBs will continue to pound the streets and lanes into their forties, fifties and beyond. Getting up at six in the morning to do so, always running on their own (God help you if you try chatting to one) and wearing the same singlet no matter how much overgrown back hair is showing. And do they enjoy it? Hardly ever.

S

SCHOOL

In 1997, the general election mantra was education, education, education. Therefore logically, in the next general election it will probably be education, education, education, even more bloody education.

COBs are aware of the importance of education – if nothing else it keeps the majority of children off the streets and out of sight, which is to be encouraged – although is there any need for so many school holidays?

COBs themselves do not tend to have fond memories of school. They either hold encyclopedic grudges for decades against teachers and fellow pupils for perceived slights at the age of nine who they can then blame for the rest of their lives, or they have blanked out all memory of their life as a small person.

This is why, other than colonic irrigation, there is little a COB dreads more than the thought of school reunions. Desperate events with desperate music for desperate people playing at one-upmanship and lying through their teeth about how well they are doing whilst checking out all those others who they were never friends with in the first place to see who looks the oldest, the baldest, the fattest and generally the most ruined.

SCIENCE FICTION

COBs do not really do science fiction. Captain Kirk going boldly where no Canadian had gone before, Dr Who and the original Daleks who could not go up stairs and Luke Skywalker fighting the Green Cross Code man with fluorescent tubes were all just about tolerated, but deep down COBs are suspicious enough of the present, so contemplating some fictional society centuries in the future is quite beyond them.

COBs are also not convinced by space exploration. Nobody been to the moon since 1973? Can they not find TV studios big enough anymore for a week's filming of papier mache moons, inappropriate shadows and a game of pitch and putt?

SCOTLAND

COBs are to be found in every country of the world, but for dourness, stubborness, ingrained Calvinism and conservatism with a small 'c', Scotland and Scots take crabbitness to a zen-like level of awkwardness, dryness, seriousness, Loch Ness and absolute refusal to be impressed by anything or anybody.

Show a Scotsman the Taj Mahal, the aurora borealis, a snow leopard and cub in the wild or Salma Hayek and the most you will ever get out of them was that it was alright.

A current example of this is Gordon Brown, Chancellor of the Exchequer and eternal Prime Minister in waiting, a man for whom no amount of re-styling, children and appearances on *GMTV*, *Richard and Judy* and *Celebrity Come Dancing* can change his image of grumpiest man in the room.

And teenage tennis star Andy Murray who is already at the age of 19 expressing taciturn tendencies that all Scottish COBs would approve of. Even smiley Sue Barker is driven to drink by one of his press conferences.

Scottish COBs have also had a long history of blaming other people and in particular England for all the woes of the world. This has resulted in Scots having a chip-on-the-shoulder inferiority complex several potatoes high when it comes to the English while at the same time retaining intellectual superiority over every other poor bugger in the world. This conundrum is best expressed by Scottish football fans singing 'Stand Up If You Hate England' whilst in a middle of a tense World Cup qualifier against a bemused Belgium.

How then would Scottish COBs react to devolution and the Scottish parliament (which most COBs voted against in the first place)? Simple. Blame has now been devolved to the new parliament and the diddies who got elected. All Scottish parliament successes are ignored and mistakes celebrated for years on end. All MSPs are considered numpties until proven otherwise and exercising your democratic franchise only encourages them.

Scotland – a historic and ancient nation of stunning scenery, breathtaking beauty and friendly, hospitable people. And how does the Scottish tourist industry promote itself? By bedecking themselves in tartan kitsch that has no connection past or present with 95% of the Scottish population. By promoting as a major tourist attraction a couple of tractor tyres in Loch Ness. And, as for bagpipes, no wonder the British army won so many wars – anything to escape that screeching racket heading towards them.

Scotland – the land so crabbit that they invented the word.

THE SEA

Dark. Deep. Forbidding. Implacable. Uncompromising. Never to be underestimated.

Yes, the only difference between COBs and the sea is that the sea is wet and used to have fish in it.

SEX

You cannot generalise a COBs attitude when it comes to exchanging bodily fluids – COBs can be as indifferent or enthusiastic as the next person.

All you can say about COBs and sex is that they tend to be quieter than most whilst in the throes of the passion and the only comment you are likely to get afterwards is the cursing that takes place when they stub their toe when going to the bathroom in the dark.

SITCOMS

Everyone talks about the golden age of British sitcoms. *Porridge*, *Dad's Army*, *Fawlty Towers*, *Blackadder*, etc, etc. How would BBC2 fill their schedules if it wasn't for all these 30-year-old repeats on constant reruns?

The problem, however, with these classic comedies

is that once you get past the select few you actually realise how unfunny most of them were. *The Good Life*, *Keeping Up Appearances*, *Open All Hours*, *Last Of The Summer Wine*, *'Allo 'Allo* and *The Young Ones* – entire episodes can come and go without any comedy or much situation for that matter.

Not that modern sitcoms are any better. *Nighty Night*, *Saxondale*, *Little Britain*, *Green Wing* etc – all so dark, bitter and post-modern that the very thought of cracking a joke is comedy heresy.

You get more laughs watching a *Newsnight* Middle East special.

SMOKING BAN

You have COBs who smoke (usually rolled tobacco) and COBs who don't. All of them are united in wondering that if smoking is so dangerous and unhealthy then why doesn't the Government just ban it altogether and do without the billions of tax and duty. That's what they hate about politicians – sanctimonious puritans unless there is money involved.

As for the smoking ban and Britain's trans-formation into a continental land of cosmopolitan cafes and outdoor gazebos – well, as any COB will tell you, the pub is an oasis of peace and reflection, a sanctuary from the outside world and not somewhere to be on display for the whole world to know your business and, more importantly, where you are.

SOAP OPERAS

COBs are particularly sniffy about what in television are now called continuing dramas. Several reasons are given for this antipathy.

1) First there's the argument that they're not as good as they were when Elsie Tanner/Annie Sugden/ Dirty Den the first time/Mrs Dale etc were in them. This, of course, ignores the fact that in the past the acting could even be worse than it is now (eg Ali Osman from *Eastenders*) and the highlight of a week of *Emmerdale Farm* was whether Jack Sugden had acquired a new pair of wellies.

2) There is the 'all they ever show on television these days is soaps' excuse. This would be legitimate if it was not for the fact that COBs are first to complain when *Corrie* is postponed by thirty minutes to make way for the exciting Champions League penalty shoot-out or tragic royal fatality.

3) There is the 'soaps are not of high dramatic quality' excuse. So we'll be seeing you at the next revival of Chekhov (the *Cherry Orchard* playwright

not the man from *Star Trek*) at your local theatre then.

4) That soaps and especially *Eastenders* are depressing and dreary, lacking in everyday warmth and humour excuse. A somewhat ironic position for COBs to take.

As far as soaps are concerned it doesn't matter whether you watch them or not – they will be on again tomorrow or the next day. If you want to know what happens, flick through one of those numerous 60p TV magazines at the newsagent. If you missed something, the plotline will be used again anyway (Ian Beale gets married, Ian Beale gets dumped, Ian Beale gets married again etc). And if you have a favourite character who gets written out of the series, don't worry, he or she will turn up in *Holby City* or *The Bill* before you know it.

SPELLING

COBs get annoyed by bad spelling. They are disappointed by those that write dissapointed. They are embarrassed for those who write embarressed. And find unacceptable anyone who writes unaccepteble. COBs feel that it is important that one should be able to correctly spell zeitgeist, archipelago and soliloquy, although find it difficult to use this knowledge when writing Christmas cards.

SPORT

As far as COBs are concerned there are only six sports that really matter. Football, horse racing, golf, cricket and rugby union and league. They find watching motor sport akin to two hours of having a mosquito in the room, tennis and snooker are watched by people with no interest in sport and boxing is on so late only insomniacs can follow it.

This is not to say COBs do not enjoy other sports. They are quite happy to shout 'DRUGS!' at the TV screen when the commentator informs you that a certain athlete or swimmer has improved his time by two seconds this season. And there is probably nothing in life that amuses COBs more than seeing figure skaters fall over.

And, to be fair to the BBC, whenever they are going to show you some sporting action that is particularly Mickey Mouse they give you plenty of warning by letting you know that the programme will be presented by perky Hazel Irvine.

STUDENTS

COBs do not have a lot of time for students. This is not just because they spend up to a decade studying the incredibly useful subjects of media studies and marketing in the numerous colleges and universities that over the past 30 years have sprung up to give degrees where they used to give swimming certificates. That is when they can bothered to study at all in between extensive drinking of cheap lager and subsidised alcopops and trying to get off with *Hollyoaks* wannabees.

No, what really annoys COBs about students is the sheer cost of them. In the old days if you came from a lower income background but had the brain and the inclination you could get a grant or a bursary. Today there are tuition fees and top-up fees and thousands and thousands of pounds of student loans and student debts to be paid off by the poor unfortunate sods who begat the workshy future of the country in the first place.

SUPERHEROES

Two of the lesser known superheroes are Crabbitman and his occasional sidekick Crabbitwoman.

Crabbitman has the power of always being right,

the power of predicting the future (Crabbitman's motto is 'I knew that was going to happen') and has worn exactly the same superhero outfit for the past 40 years.

Crabbitwoman is known for her glacial expression, her ability to fly, which enables her to look down on everybody, and when angry she turns a severe shade of navy blue.

SUPERMODELS

COBs are totally unconvinced about why young women impersonating startled giraffes get paid millions of pounds for sullenly walking in a straight line, turning up late and avoiding puddings.

At least you can argue that your old-style supermodels made the clothes look good and rock stars happy, but you do fear for the noses of the new, even younger and skinnier models who you expect would not deal well with a strong gust of wind.

T

TAXIS

COBs are not fond of being in taxis. In the first instance somebody else is driving. Secondly, they are dependent on this other person knowing where they are going and not taking the scenic route. Thirdly, there is the whole question of how much it costs to get from A to B in a straight line without hitting anything. And does one tip? And if so, how much does one tip etc etc.

The whole taxi situation is exacerbated when COBs are abroad – for no matter how genial and friendly the local taxi driver, the overriding fear is still one of losing all one's money and being sold into slavery.

TERRORISM

COBs are all in favour of the war on terror. Better to arrest them all, interrogate them, lock them up, throw away the key, whatever it takes, as it is better that a few innocents lose their freedom for the greater good that the majority are protected from the forces of death and destruction. And once you have interned all the Irish, then you can move on to other nationalities as well.

TIGERS

Difficult to know what is more infuriating – the hunters that shoot tigers, the traffickers who sell them, the Indian government for losing all the tigers they were supposed to be protecting or Kelloggs continuing to have bloody Tony the Tiger saying everything's grrrreat – when clearly it is not.

We can put a man on the moon, make seventy-year-old women pregnant and invent computers smaller than your fingernail, so why on earth can't we keep a few stripey cats in the jungle alive?

TIME

COBs can be very specific about time. They get up at a certain time and go to bed at a certain time. Eggs should boil for a consistent number of minutes. Digestives should be eaten at stated times. Journeys should have an optimum timescale from departure to arrival. Jobs should take the same amount of time to complete, never more, never less. Evening meals should never begin any later than 6.30. And the entire rhythm and routine of a week can be disrupted by ITV incomprehensibly scheduling *Emmerdale* at ten o'clock in the evening.

When it comes to watches – other than knowing that gold and Mickey Mouse are unacceptable in all circumstances – COBs have no interest in designer brands but just want something that works. As for clocks, COBs have dozens of them, which makes the beginning and ending of British Summer Time a particularly stressful time to ensure that every one is accurate. COBs feel mental anguish at the mere sight of a clock that has stopped. The concept of time standing still and life going on forever is just too painful a prospect to contemplate.

TOLKIEN

The great advantage of Peter Jackson's award-winning *Lord Of the Rings* trilogy was that it meant never having to read the books. It is often said that half the world have read Tolkien and the other half have yet to. Well, COBs were in the half that had not read Tolkien and now they won't bother. Even giving up nearly 12 hours of your life to watch the movies felt like several days too long.

TOP OF THE POPS

Why on earth has the BBC axed *Top Of The Pops* after 42 years? Did they not realise after the whole *One Man And His Dog* debacle that people get annoyed when they stop making long-running programmes? Unless of course it is *Last Of The Summer Wine*, although even here can anyone actually prove that they have not been repeating the same programme for the past 25 years?

Not that COBs actually have any intention of watching *Top Of the Pops*. They either stopped watching in 1971 when Marc Bolan wore glitter, in 1978 when Siouxsie Sioux stopped wearing bondage, in 1995 when Keith Flint of The Prodigy scared the bejasus out of them or in 1987 at the sheer injustice of 'Fairytale Of New York' by The Pogues not being Christmas Number One.

COBs, however, intrinsically believe that programmes such as *Top Of the Pops*, *Blue Peter* and *The Sky At Night* are the reason that they pay their licence fee. So that the BBC can, year after year, make programmes that they never watch, but feel reassured at their continued existence. And, when all is said and done, there must be more potential viewers for *Top Of the Pops* than watch the smug gits on *Eggheads* every night, where the only tension is whether Chris and Kevin actually start licking themselves.

TRAVEL

You would think that COBs would enjoy travel. They are happy to share their thoughts and experiences of many issues concerning many parts of the globe that they appear well acquainted with. The foreign policy of George W. Bush, the expansion of the European Union, the historical influence of Islam, the merits of the growing customer services market of the Indian sub-continent and the politics of Africa are but a selection of the international issues of the day that COBs can discuss with passion and vigour.

And it would be wrong to criticise COBs for having views about places that they know nothing about. This would be unfair as COBs have travelled extensively. They have been to America (Orlando), Asia (Singapore), Africa (the Pyramids), Eastern Europe (Prague) and the Middle East (Cyprus), so they know what they're talking about. And as for Europe, who better to express an opinion on the introduction of the Euro and the reform of the Common Agricultural Policy than somebody who has travelled extensively through Greece and Spain.

Younger COBs are also well-versed to discuss the many issues concerning modern Europe after having gone interrailing for a month in 1986.

TRUST

As Fox Mulder said – trust no one, except perhaps your family, of whom you should still remain suspicious. The exceptions to this rule are David Attenbrough (who seems fairly reliable) and your pets – who are good at keeping secrets, unless you have a talking budgie.

U

U2

When it comes to pop stars that COBs cannot be doing with, one group are head and shoulders above the rest. Of the main contenders, Madonna is like Hadrian's Wall – been around forever, quite impressive in its construction, but not something you give much thought to. Jim Kerr and Simple Minds only bellow away to family and friends these days and you only have to put up with Sir Bob Geldof's moaning once every decade. Most COBs have yet to encounter the sheer tedium of the Red Hot Chilli Peppers. This leaves U2 as remaining consistently average, overblown and self-important for the last 25 years, making millions, waving flags and wearing hats, as The Edge plays interminable guitar solos and Bono travels the globe having his photo taken with world leaders. As they sang in 1983 'This Is Not A Rebel Song', and not much has changed since.

V

VINEGAR

In recent years there has been a remarkable upsurge in sales of vinegar and books on vinegar. When analysing these sales, most are to COBs who appreciate vinegar for its adaptability as a product that can be used in cooking, as a cleanser and has cleaning properties as well. Non-COBs are not surprised by COBs approval of vinegar as it helps explain their permanently sour countenance.

W

WAR

Hoouuuh! What is it good for? Well COBs believe in the concept of war. Defence of kith and kin and defence of the innocent and oppressed are honourable if regrettable courses of action for a nation to enter into. To paraphrase the Blues Brothers and Heaven 17, COBs have no time for Nazis and those that attempt to exonerate them with such flimsy drivel as the trains ran on time etc.

Older COBs may well have experienced military service themselves and are well aware of the randomness and cruelty of conflict and that victory is not to be glorified but an acknowledgement that the killing has come to an end.

So when it comes to war, by all means defend your nation and support the oppressed, but when you ask your country for approval in sending our army to invade and occupy another country:

a) Try not to fabricate the reasons for doing so to make your case better.

b) Don't then come up with some new reasons when the first reasons prove not to be true.

c) Above all, have some semblance of a plan of what to do next if you actually manage to occupy said country.

In general it is one thing for a government to be deceitful and economical with the *actualité* (we don't really expect anything else) but being incompetent is just poor.

Anyway, on the positive side, thanks be that there never were any weapons of mass destruction in Iraq. If you truly want to balls things up for the rest of the century then invasion of Iran and Syria would do the trick.

THE WEATHER

Of all the many facets that make up a COB it is a COBs relationship with the weather that is particularly pronounced.

Weather is either too cold, too wet, too dry or too hot. Summers are too short, winters are too long. Weather was much better when we were younger, and with global warming we are all doomed anyway.

If COBs find the concept of a nice day out somewhat alien, what truly infuriates them (and this is especially true of COBs of a Northern persuasion) is the new BBC weather map which shrinks Scotland to the size of Kent and loses the Scottish islands altogether whilst keeping most of Northern France and Belgium. And to make things even worse they don't even bother telling you the weather in Dieppe and Le Havre if you fancy nipping over for a truckful of Cabernet.

WINE

Wine, wine and more wine. One moment you are savouring (if it's not too sacrilegious) a Blue Nun and happy with your glass of Shloer, the next, you have just about got your head around the concept of ordering a bottle of house white and house red and not to mix the two in the same glass, and before you know it you have to know your Pinots from your Sauvignon Blancs and your Chablis from your cheeky little Merlots.

Now it's tricky enough ordering wine from a wine list – all extortionately priced but probably palatable, but when it comes to selecting from an off-licence it becomes nigh-on impossible. Even when you exclude all the Chardonnays you are still left with a choice of hundreds with absolutely no chance of remembering what that nice Chilean you had last time was.

Furthermore, how much are you supposed to pay? £3.99 is clearly too cheap for a good bottle of wine and unquestionably either undrinkable or Australian or probably both, while anything over £5.99 is extravagant in the extreme. And as for bubbly, be very, very careful indeed – the cork could have someone's eye out.

WORLD RECORDS

COBs are dismissive of modern day exceptional human achievements. Mountaineers and explorers are categorised as posh boys and girls who cannot handle real life and therefore spend thousands of pounds of daddy's money trying to find new ways of inflicting as much physical and mental pain on themselves as possible. Unbalanced the lot of them.

Now your real explorers, your Captain Scotts, your Ernest Shackletons, your Edmund Hillarys, were probably as unhinged (although having said that it would be unlikely that any of them would have as many frozen sandwiches missing from an Arctic picnic as Ranulph Fiennes appears to) but they didn't have computers, camera crews, mobile phones and modern clothing to discover the ends of the world. No, all they had were a stiff upper lip, a pipe, copious amounts of tea, some unfortunate dogs and a nice woolly jumper that their wife had knitted for them.

Poor unfortunate Ellen Macarthur in particular receives the ire of COBs. Why does she need to keep sailing around the world all the time, they ask – hasn't she been everywhere by now? Why does she always have to go sailing on her own – has she got no friends? And what's with all the crying in force 10 hurricanes – doesn't she listen to the weather forecast?

X

X FACTOR

COBs have long suspected that years ago breweries, pubs and clubs got together with the television companies and agreed to give them billions of pounds in perpetuity to make Saturday night television as dreadful as possible so that people would be forced to go out.

Even now, long after the damage has been done, the BBC and ITV still spend millions on some poor unfortunate, untalented diddy, give them a Saturday show and see their careers go down the tubes eighteen months later. Step forward Brian Conley, Anthea Turner, Vernon Kay and Graham Norton amongst others.

And that is before you get to the torture of the talent shows where members of the public who have never done a proper day's work in their lives get humiliated by the musical geniuses who gave the world Robson & Jerome and Boyzone in their desperate attempts to become the next Gareth Gates.

Binge drinking or a double bill of *Celebrity Ice Dancing* and *How Do You Solve A Problem Like Maria*? No contest really.

Y

YOGHURT

Or yoghurt multi-packs to be exact. In principle a grand idea to have a variety of four different and exciting flavours all at a good value price. And then they go and ruin it by making the fourth one vanilla or red cherry. The same principle, of course, used to apply with crisps and the cruel inclusion of beef in all multi-packs.

Z

ZZZZZ

After a hard day of complaining and moaning, of feeling irritable and disappointed by everyone and everything around them, it is time for our COBs to go to sleep.

Do our COBs sleep soundly? Yes they do.

Do they dream of fluffy kittens, beautiful sunsets and romantic liaisons with sun-kissed senors and senoritas? Who knows – they never say.

And finally, some handy hints and reminders about the likes and dislikes of the COB, workplace issues, COB bosses and the age-old question of whether or not it is nobler to be a COB.

25 THINGS THAT COBS CAN JUST ABOUT TOLERATE

Sheep
Porridge
Wakes
BBC nature programmes
Otters
An open fire
Garden centres
Cathedrals
Fishing
People with a talent for ironing
The aurora borealis
The Lake District
The Hitchhiker's Guide to the Galaxy (but only the radio series)
A hot drink before bedtime
The Red Cross

Boats in a harbour
Lighthouses
Eight hours uninterrupted sleep
That brief moment of optimism when spring has
  sprung
Comfortable pants
The TV series *House*
Remembrance Day
Tap water
The University of Life
I'm Sorry I Haven't A Clue

25 THINGS THAT COBS SIMPLY CANNOT BE DOING WITH

Babies wearing baseball caps
'Angels' by Robbie Williams being sung in public
Civilian deaths being described as collateral damage
Runny scrambled eggs
Overhanging stomachs on public display
Attempting to locate the G-spot
The myth that free personal care for the elderly is
   going to last
Bean bags
Politicians saying that they are tough on crime
   and tough on the causes of crime
Valentine's Day
Wedding lists
Junk mail
Vanessa Feltz
Noisy breakfast radio DJs
Anybody who writes their autobiography before
   the age of 30
Dick & Dom in da Bungalow
No legroom on planes
No cricket on real TV
Fellow Brits on beach holidays
People who shriek

Fireworks
Robert Mugabe
Straws and accoutrements in your drink
Graduates who can't change a plug
Teenagers who can't hold their drink

HOW A COBBY BOSS
MOTIVATES THEIR STAFF

Your staff are both individuals and a team working together.
Encourage your team by treating all individuals equally grumpily – therefore generating a team spirit united against you.

Always be willing to challenge your staff.
Delegate responsibility so that, ideally, your staff can do all the work. If a task is successfully completed, remember to make the next task more difficult. If a task is unsuccessfully completed, remember to shout at as many people as possible.

Always communicate with clarity.
Initially, and to avoid any misunderstanding, this should be done verbally in as loud a voice as possible. Verbal communication, however, should always be followed up with written confirmation in clear concise bullet points of all the areas where your staff have gone wrong. Remember that full knowledge of the facts should not get in the way of a good bollocking.

Humour and fun are essential parts of the work environment.

You should wear a paper hat at the Christmas party to show your lighter side. For the rest of the year however it is important to be consistent and therefore it is vital that you are always as grim as possible so that staff know where they are.

Involve your staff in recruitment.

As one look at your miserable mug might put people off, it is always good to delegate the recruitment to others. However, as a manager it is your responsibility should you need to let any members of staff go – although it is apparently deemed inappropriate to look as if you are actually enjoying firing someone.

TO BE OR NOT TO BE A COB

So where does this leave us? Clearly COBs are not solely defined by gender, nationality, class or creed. Even age is not a defining factor as you can have your grumpy, dour teenagers as well as your cheerful, good-natured pensioners.

What would seem conclusive, however, is that crabbitness is not an attractive trait in a person. Grim, negative, unhelpful, unimpressed by everything and everybody, COBs are not what could be classified as little rays of sunshine. If you are looking for humour, support and generosity of spirit then you have come to the wrong place.

Yet when all is said and done – and at the end of the day –and after a game of two halves – and after leaving no cliché unturned – do we not admire our COBs for their consistency, their sarcasm, their dependability and, as Gorgeous George once said, their indefatabagility?

In a society gripped by political correctness, political spin, insincerity, obesity, emotional constipation, intellectual dumbing down, eighty-eight channels of all-day cartoons and reality TV and shrieking women driving round cities in pink fire engines, is it not essential that there are COBs amongst us to rail against mediocrity, who are willing to call a spade a bloody big shovel.

So, if you know a crabbit old bugger, respect them, love them, treasure them, tolerate them, make them cups of teas, buy them Jaffa Cakes, let them read the paper in peace. For deep down, despite all appearances, deep down they probably love you too.

CRABBIT OLD BUGGERS

JOHN K V EUNSON is well-known for his crabbit tendencies. He has been crabbit almost his whole life and has become increasingly grumpy as the years go by. His interests include sheep, quality television and a hot drink before bedtime. He lives in his own head.

Also by John K V Eunson

Sheep for Beginners – A dip into the world of wool